the allotment book

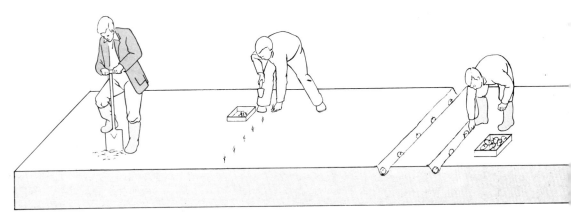

SAMPSON LOW

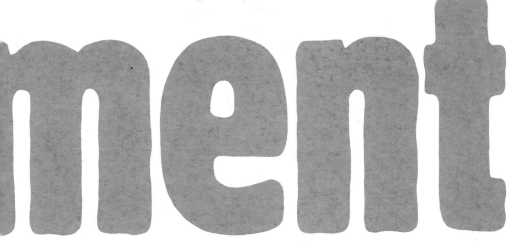

ment

a visual guide
to successful growing
by the DIAGRAM GROUP

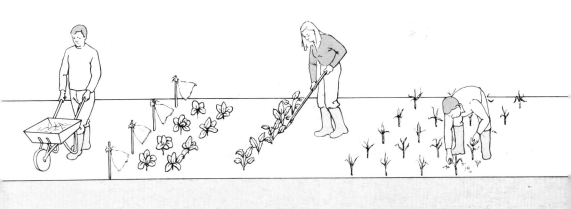

Warning

The advice given in this book covers general rules. So read the instructions on seed packets, because there are many different kinds of seeds, which may have their own peculiarities.

Always read and follow carefully the instructions on fertilisers, pest controls, insecticides etc *before* using.

Wash out carefully buckets, syringes etc that have been used for fertilisers or insecticides. Also wash pots well before re-using. If they are clay, soak them before filling with soil.

Clean off spades, forks, and other tools after use.

If you buy bedding-out plants, buy from a reputable nurseryman.

Keep the allotment clear of rubbish, which harbours such pests as slugs and woodlice.

First published in 1977 by
Sampson Low, Berkshire House
Queen Street, Maidenhead,
Berkshire SL6 1NF

© Diagram Visual Information Ltd.
All rights reserved
Printed by Purnell & Sons Ltd

SBN 562 00069 0

Don't throw away all your empty peat and fertiliser bags. They may prove useful for storage or other purposes.

Mark and record your seed rows clearly. The beginner, particularly, may not recognise seedlings when they come. You won't remember where you put things, although you think you will.

It is the weather, rather than the calendar, that affects growth. The sowing dates etc given in the book or on the packet are based on normal seasonal weather, and common sense calls for slight adjustments when it is unseasonal or in northern, colder conditions.

Don't forget that if the allotment feeds you, you must feed it. The nourishment that your vegetables have taken out has to be replaced by compost, manure, fertilisers etc.

The Diagram Group

Editor   Bernard Cleves

Assistant Editors   Maureen Cartwright, Elizabeth Wilhide

Art Editor   Richard Hummerstone

Artists   Jeff Alger, Eileen Batterberry, Stephen Clark, Robert Galvin, Brian Hewson, Susan Kinsey, Roger Kohn, Pavel Kostal, Janos Marffy, Graham Rosewarne, Diana Taylor.

Consultants   R. Bounford, H. Elesmore

Picture credits   Greater London Photographic Library
Radio Times, Hulton Picture Library
Ken Coton. Pamla Toler

dedicated to E.M.

Contents

7   Warning to readers
8   Introduction
16   Glossary
18   **Chapter one: Setting out**
20   Starting from scratch
22   Weeds and their treatment
24   Planning your plot
26   Down to earth
28   Give us the tools
30   Storing your tools
32   Sent to try us
34   Trench warfare
36   Under glass
38   Cloches
40   Greenhouses
42   Feeding your plot
44   Back to the land – compost
46   **Chapter two: Growing plans**
48   Planning the year
52   Keeping your distance
54   The rotation of crops
56   Sowing in the open
58   Taking root
60   What to hope for

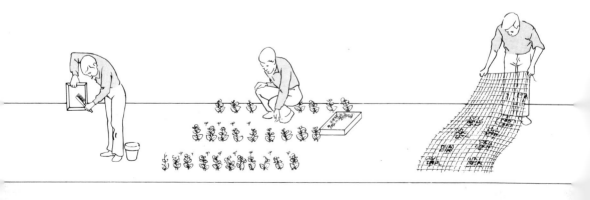

62 **Chapter three: Vegetables**

64 Brassicas: Cabbage, Brussels sprouts, Broccoli, Cauliflower, Kale

70 Leaf vegetables: Lettuce, Spinach, Celtuce, Corn Salad, Sorrel, Swiss Chard, Good King Henry, Endive, Mustard and Cress

74 Root and Tuber vegetables: Carrot, Beetroot, Parsnip, Turnip, Radish, Potato, other root and tuber vegetables

84 Seed vegetables: Beans, Peas, Sweet corn

90 Bulb and stalk vegetables: Leek, Onion, Garlic, Shallot, Celery, Rhubarb, Seakale, Asparagus, Chicory, Globe artichoke, Cardoon, Finnochio

100 Vegetable fruits: Tomato, Marrow, Cucumber, Sweet pepper, Courgette, Pumpkin, Aubergine

106 Herbs

110 Friend or foe

114 **Chapter four: Fruits of your labour**

116 Training fruit

118 Soft fruits

122 Fruit trees

126 Methods of storing: Outdoors, Indoors, Bottling, Jams, Jellies, Pickles and chutneys, Freezing vegetables and fruit

138 From garden to allotment

140 On the record

142 Index

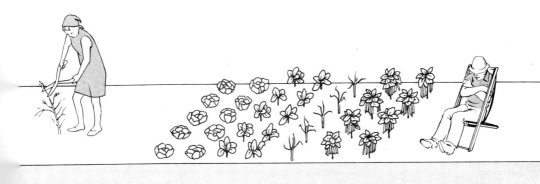

About the book

Children enjoy helping in the allotment, and can learn by experience how their food is produced.

The purpose of this book is not just to initiate the novice into the skills of vegetable growing but to bring together in an easy to understand and easy to find form the knowledge that is essential for every gardener. The book takes the reader through from the moment that he acquires his plot to the time when, we hope, he loads his shelves and freezer with the fruits of his labours and stands gazing, with justifiable pride, at his stores of potatoes and vegetables that will last him through the winter.

The book starts, literally, from scratch: from the moment when you take over an allotment that, let's face it, may well have been sadly neglected. It tells you the sort of tools and other equipment you need, the types of soil you may encounter and what to do about them, how to plan, dig and prepare the plot. The next section covers such details as when to sow, when to expect to see the first gratifying tips of green in your seed rows, and when you can expect to harvest the crops. It tells about sowing in the open and under glass, the rotation of crops and what you can expect in the way of yields.

The next section moves on to the actual practice of growing. All common, and many uncommon, vegetables are dealt with separately; how they are sown or planted, the soil they prefer, how they are cultivated etc. Then, assuming that you have enough space on your allotment for some fruit, the book deals briefly but informatively with the basic problems of growing modest quantities of hard and soft fruits. Finally, having taken you through the growing cycle, the book explains how to preserve, store or freeze the vegetables and fruit you have grown. Scattered throughout the book are a number of tips of the trade that have been devised by gardeners through the ages.

If you follow the few simple rules, you have more than a sporting chance of becoming a life member of the Greenfingers Club, a healthier person and a benefactor to yourself, your family and your purse. But this is a sensible book about vegetable growing and there are three things that have to be taken into account. You must have the land on which to grow, the knowledge with which to grow, and (most important of all) the willingness to put in the hard and continuing work that the successful growing of vegetables involves. The planning and cultivation of a vegetable plot truly do call for devotion and steady work, and the fact that it is infinitely rewarding, satisfying both a primitive urge to create and the baser appetites too, does not alter the fact that it is not easy.

Confucius he say
He wasn't talking about Chinese cabbage but it is better to water soil before sowing seeds than to wash them out by overhead watering afterwards.

Why grow your own?

There is a saying 'as like as two peas.' Nothing could be further from the truth, for there is a wide variety of peas, which grow, look and taste differently. But nowhere is the difference so great as between freshly picked peas grown on your own allotment and canned, packaged or frozen peas bought in a store or market, or for that matter peas in the pod bought from your greengrocer.

This is true of every vegetable. Tender young carrots straight from the soil, crisp, green, hearty lettuces still warm from the evening sun, and long, succulent runner beans seem to come from a different world than the often limp and sad offerings in the shops. And so they do. But don't blame the greengrocer. The fact is that his vegetables are long dead, and may have travelled hundreds of miles, before getting into your shopping bag, let alone on to your table!

And the price! Provided that you strove for succession the average-sized family might just be able, throughout the summer months, to eat the lettuces from one seed packet costing less than 20p. Yet there are plenty of times during the year when you can pay over twice that amount for a single lettuce. Take brussels sprouts or new potatoes. For the price of only one seed you can hope for up to 2 lb (0.9 kg) of brussels sprouts. And 5 lb (2.3 kg) of seed potatoes should give 40–60 lb (18–27 kg) of potatoes when you harvest.

Don't forget that not only can you grow food cheaply, but you can also grow what you want, in and often out of season. There's no doubt about the economics of having your own vegetable garden and every reason why what you grow should be infinitely better than what you usually buy.

Allotments in the UK

In 1975, about 51,625 acres of England and Wales were devoted to allotments. This may seem a high figure although it equals only 1 acre in roughly every 719 acres in the two countries. Yet it has been much higher, for at the end of World War II there were over twice as many acres (107,282) under allotment cultivation, or 1 acre in every 345 of the total area. But the true figure for 1975 is nearer 1 acre in every 227 if we consider only *cultivated* land.

As can be seen from the table below, the number of allotments has always increased at times of national crisis. By the end of World War I it had increased tenfold. During World War II it went up by about 300%. Other influences in the past have included the industrialisation of towns, with populations moving away from the countryside but still wanting their home-grown vegetables, and the increase in the number of council houses (which at the time reduced the number of allotments).

It can reasonably be said that the strips of land provided by the lord of the manor for his villeins under the feudal system were basically a form of allotment, as were also the common lands they shared. Many of the strips were lost by the villeins, paradoxically enough, as they gained their freedom, and throughout the centuries many of the common lands were lost by enclosure. By the end of the 19th century, allotments had begun to be treated seriously and various Allotments Acts had been passed by Parliament. These were consolidated in the Small Holdings and Allotments Act of 1908, which rules today although there have been a number of qualifying Acts since. The main purpose of the Acts was to define the relations between allotment landlords and tenants and to establish under whose authority they would be run.

This table shows the fluctuations in numbers of allotments.

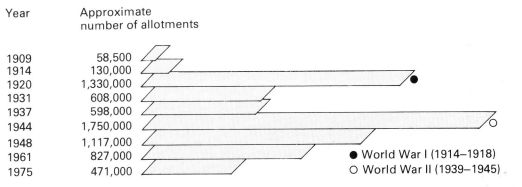

Year	Approximate number of allotments
1909	58,500
1914	130,000
1920	1,330,000
1931	608,000
1937	598,000
1944	1,750,000
1948	1,117,000
1961	827,000
1975	471,000

● World War I (1914–1918)
○ World War II (1939–1945)

The Allotments World

There are many laws concerning allotments and the new holder should not delay in joining any local association of allotment holders, which will be able to advise him not only on practical growing problems but particularly on legal matters. It is only possible here to touch on a few of the legal problems.

Usually written tenancy agreements are for a year, renewable from year to year afterwards, and are signed by an authorised officer of the local Council as landlord and by the allotment holder as tenant. Continuity of occupation is important, especially if long-term fruit trees, for example, are being planted. Sometimes the agreement requires the tenant to relinquish the holding if he moves from the district.

Common to most agreements are the requirements that the tenant should keep fences etc in good repair, not cause nuisance to neighbouring holders, not erect buildings without permission and keep the allotment well cultivated (e.g. clear of weeds). The agreement may forbid the keeping of animals such as hens and rabbits without prior consent. Rent is usually paid quarterly in advance.

There are two forms of local association: those that own land and whose member are the tenants of the allotments on it, and those formed by allotment holders grouping together to protect their own interests and perhaps share their experiences. The former have a legal entity, the others do not, but their activities are centralised under a national organisation, the National Society of Leisure Gardeners Ltd, formerly the National Allotments and Gardens Society Ltd. Among its activities are fire insurance schemes, discount facilities for seeds, fertilisers etc and the provision of advice to its members and to local authorities on all matters relating to allotments.

If you are seeking an allotment the best thing to do is to apply to your local Council (usually the Parks and Recreation Department). Rents vary from one district to another, and for a 300 square yard plot you might have to pay £15 per year (you should certainly have water laid on for this) or as little as £2 per year. Allotments systems vary in different parts of the world. In the suburbs of Berlin, for instance, there are some 40,000 allotments. Most of them were created at the end of World War II partly to keep people away from the bombed areas of the city. They are at least twice the size of their British equivalents, and often have residential chalets that can be used as weekend cottages, and a communal clubhouse where the allotment holders can relax. France and the Netherlands are among other European countries with allotment schemes. In the USA there is no national organisation of allotments but 'community gardens,' as they are called there, are increasing in number. Pennsylvania is organising a state scheme, and some large firms allocate spare land to their employees for allotment growing. Other states and cities have youth garden programmes, often attached to schools.

far left
Many allotments are the exploitation of otherwise wasted land. Railway embankments are particularly suitable.

So when you choose your allotment, if you have a choice, do be sensible. Check on the sort of soil it has. Look at its size and ask yourself whether you really can handle it; whether you are prepared to give up most of your spare time to it; whether it might not be better to get someone to share it with you. How far is it from your home, walking, by car or by public transport? Don't forget that you may have to get bags of peat and fertiliser there and that you hope to have to bring back sacks of potatoes, boxes of apples etc. Is there water laid on? Water is heavy stuff to transport in a drought. It will be nice, but not all that usual, to inherit a small greenhouse: there will almost certainly be a shed of some sort but it may not be much more than an overgrown tool cupboard.

Allotments vary in size. They are generally divided into 10 rod plots (i.e. about 300 square yards) and few exceed 40 rods, which is the size mentioned in the Allotments Act of 1922. This defines an 'allotment garden' as 'an allotment not exceeding 40 poles in extent which is wholly or mainly cultivated by the occupier for the production of vegetable or fruit crops for consumption by himself or his family'. For the benefit of those who have forgotten their old-fashioned square measure, a rod and a pole are the same thing, measuring just over 30 square yards. (The average size of an allotment at the end of World War II was about 484 square yards or roughly 16 rods). Most, but not all, allotments are administered by local authorities under the very loose control of the Department of the Environment. Many allotments are also provided on spare land owned by British Rail and the National Coal Board.

Allotments and gardens

Although this book is meant for allotment holders the guidance on cultivation etc. applies equally, of course, to growing vegetables in your own garden. Gardens have both advantages and disadvantages compared with allotments. To begin with they are not necessarily of the same neat rectangular shape as allotments and they are more liable to be over-shadowed by neighbouring houses or trees. Moreover, whereas an allotment is generally a strictly utilitarian operation designed to produce edible vegetation, the garden places greater emphasis on appearance, with lawns and herbaceous borders staking rival claims to those of the humble onions or carrots.

On the other hand gardens do have some considerable advantages. Usually the question of water does not arise. If it is not laid on in the garden itself, it is available in the house. Whether you have sheds or greenhouses or not, your house is immediately adjacent for shelter in rough weather, and you can take advantage of short, fine spells in the spring to slip out and do a few jobs. With an allotment, involving a journey from and to your home, it is usually a question of putting in a few hours or none at all.

It may well be worth taking a look at your garden and considering whether, in these hard times, a few alterations might not allow you to produce a worthwhile quantity of vegetables. A bit off the lawn, or altering a bed or two could do the trick.

Improvisation, the master skill of an allotment holder, can turn old doors, windows, and timber, into sheds, hotframes, and fences.

Glossary

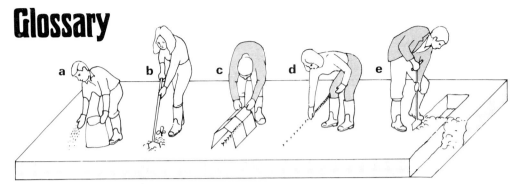

Annuals	Plants that grow and mature in one year.
Biennials	Plants whose life cycle covers two years.
Blanching	The process of whitening the stems or leaves of plants, e.g. celery and endive. Also used to describe the preparation of vegetables for freezing by plunging them in boiling water.
Bolting	Vegetables flowering or seeding prematurely.
Brassicas	The members of the cabbage family, including brussels sprouts, cauliflowers etc.
Catch Cropping	Also known as inter-cropping. The practice of growing fast-maturing crops between slow-maturing ones. The former are out of the way by the time the others are fully grown.
Cloche	A portable glass or plastic cover, usually bell- or tent-shaped placed over vegetables to protect them and speed up growth.
Compost	Humus made in the garden from decayed vegetable matter, chemicals and soil. The name is also applied to specially prepared mixtures of soil and chemicals for sowing and potting.
Dressing	Top-dressing: an application of fertiliser scattered on the surface and raked or hoed in. Base-dressing: an application of humus dug into the soil before planting out. (**a**)
Earthing up	The practice of drawing soil up around plants to blanch or protect them. (**b**)
Fertilisers	Organic or inorganic preparations used to improve the fertility of the soil.
Forcing	Encouraging the hastening of plants to maturity usually by growing under glass in some way. (**c**)
Half-Hardy	Plants that cannot survive in low temperatures.
Hardening off	Preparing greenhouse-grown seedlings for planting out by gradually introducing them to more rigorous conditions.

Haulms The stems or stalks of potatoes, beans, peas etc.

Heeling in Planting temporarily in the ground, usually pending planting out in permanent positions.

Humus The valuable dark brown result of the decomposition of vegetable matter.

Lights The name given to greenhouse windows and the translucent tops of garden frames.

Maiden The young apple or pear tree in its first year before pruning.

Mulching Covering the soil around plants with some form of organic matter to keep it moist and prevent weed growth.

Perennials Plants that remain alive over a number of years.

Pricking out Separating young seedlings to avoid overcrowding and in preparation for planting out in permanent sites.

Pruning The removal of superfluous growth in branches and twigs to promote greater fruitfulness.

Rotation of Crops The system of regularly changing the area on which particular crops are grown, to avoid soil exhaustion and the perpetuation of disease.

Stopping Pinching out the growing points to stop further upward growth and thus encourage fuller growth below.

Successional Sowing Sowing at intervals to ensure a continuation of crops throughout the season.

Suckers Shoots that grow from below soil level, often originating in the roots rather than the stem

Thinning out Pulling out seedlings from the rows to ensure that those remaining are regularly and properly spaced out. (d)

Tilth The fine growing surface resulting from digging, hoeing and raking.

Trace elements The tiny quantities of chemicals that help to make up the soil and are essential for plant growth.

Transplanting Moving plants, usually when quite young, from one place to another.

Trenching The system of digging ground in a series of shallow trenches, filling with soil from the previous excavation. (e)

Truss A cluster of flowers or fruit growing from the main stem, as with tomatoes.

Tuber The swollen outgrowth of a stem or rhizome, such as the potato.

Chapter one
Setting out

'A garden is a lovesome thing, God wot' wrote the poet, but it may well be that your new allotment may seem to be for a while a loathsome rather than a lovesome thing. To begin with it may not be new at all but old and perhaps badly neglected over the years. And if it is new you have the problem of breaking up hitherto uncultivated land. So not for nothing is this chapter called 'Starting from Scratch', for it deals with the basic nitty-gritty of an allotment and in more ways than one may bring you down to earth.

It tells you how to tidy up your allotment; how to dispose of weeds; how to plan your beds; how to find out what kind of soil you have and what to do about it when you know; what

tools you need and how to use them. You can
learn about fertilisers and making compost,
about growing 'under glass', whether under
jamjars, in cold or hot frames or in the luxury of
a greenhouse.

There is information about the gardener's
two- and four-legged enemies and those who
don't have any legs at all. But don't let yourself
get depressed. Most gardeners like to take over
an allotment in the autumn, which is the
beginning of the annual tidying-up period
anyway. Autumn and winter are also the time
for digging and manuring and, like this chapter,
are an introduction to the later rewarding
business of sowing, growing and harvesting.

During World Wars I & II,
public parks in most
European cities were turned
over to allotment groups to
produce much needed
vegetables.

Starting from scratch

It is rarely possible to choose exactly the allotment site you would like. The nearer your home the better, for it means less travel and is safer from marauders. Most important of all is the situation and its soil. Preferably it should be rectangular with the greatest length from east to west. A very gentle slope to the south is ideal but it should not be too steep or the water will drain away. If the soil is medium loam you will have struck lucky (see pages 26–27). Now is the chance to find out what you have got.

There may already be man-made features on the site and you should consider carefully before removing them. Fences, gates (1) etc will be normal 'fixtures' but there may already be paths (2) you will want to keep, and it is unlikely that you will want to remove sheds or greenhouses (3 and 4). The sites of your compost heap (5) and bonfire (6) can be moved as you wish.

The natural features of your plot may be controllable to some extent or not. You can alter the slope (7) by terracing, and in time the soil (8). If there are trees on the plot there may be a problem with roots (9). Drainage could also be a problem if the ground is waterlogged (10) and weeds (11) will certainly have to be cleared.

Beware of short-lease allotments or temporary gardens. If you are going to do all the work of clearing up, getting rid of weeds, stones and rubbish and perhaps putting in some drainage, you certainly want to reap some harvests from it. Some vegetables do not mature for many months after sowing. It is only fair that you should be able to look forward to some years of crops.

If you have a choice in the size of your allotment, don't take on more land than you can handle. It may be that if you take over a neglected plot you can negotiate a reduction in the rent for a period, for a neglected plot may not be much easier than uncultivated land to clear. If perennial weeds such as docks, thistles, ground elder and bindweed have taken over there's a hard slog ahead, for you can't turn them in as you can grass. Fortunately a previously cultivated plot will probably have been cleared of stones and other solid rubbish.

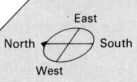

If you suspect that your allotment is too wet, sink a hole in the lowest part and see how long water remains in it. If water is excessive your plant roots may be deprived of air and the plants die.

Weeds and their treatment

One of the first jobs is to clear your plot of weeds, and the next to keep it clear. Weeds come in two sorts, annuals and perennials, and the latter are the more serious problem. The annuals can be pulled by hand or hoed out and put on the compost. They can also be dug into the soil as green manure, but only if they have not flowered: if they have, then burn them or they may seed again. With perennial weeds the best thing is to dig them up, roots and all, and burn them. When digging pick out and burn every piece of root you find.

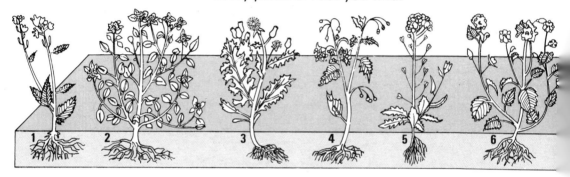

The annual weeds tend to have rather attractive country-sounding names. Above are the most common ones.

1 Charlock, also called Wild Mustard, has yellow flowers.

2 Chickweed is a bushy plant with star-shaped white flowers.

3 Groundsel is rather like a small thistle with yellow flowers.

4 Black Nightshade has white flowers and small black berries which are poisonous.

5 Shepherd's Purse, sometimes called 'salt and pepper', produces flat seed pouches rather like purses.

6 Speedwell has broad leaves not unlike a strawberry's, and bright blue flowers.

Although the twelve most common weeds are shown here, there are many others too. In *your* allotment, you may find that ragwort, horsetail or oxalis is a major problem. Try to get rid of your weeds before they seed, or you will have even more to cope with later.

Don't forget that regular mulching between rows helps to keep weeds down. So does cutting them down with a hoe. This is best done in hot weather so that the weeds die before re-rooting. Don't use a mechanical cultivator if you have any couch grass or docks in your plot. It will chop the roots into nice little pieces, each of which will produce more weeds.

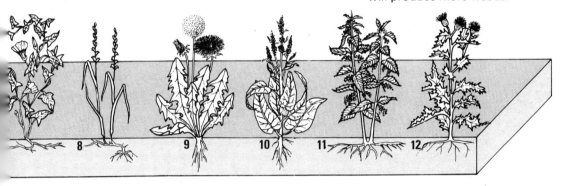

The perennial weeds often spread by means of long creeping roots. Some of the most common ones are shown above.

7   Bindweed is a type of convolvulus with spreading, creeping roots.

8   Couch, also called Quitch or Twitch, is a grass with long creeping roots with rhizomes.

9   Dandelion has widely toothed leaves (hence its name), yellow flowers and a long straight root.

10   Dock is large-leaved, and very deeply rooted if allowed to grow to any size.

11   Nettle is tall, broad-leaved, with grey-white flowers, and creeping roots which spread rapidly.

12   Creeping Thistle has a fleshy stem with prickly leaves, purple flowers and creeping roots.

It can be very dangerous to use weedkiller in the vegetable garden for obvious reasons, but sodium chlorate—2 lb (0.9 kg) in 5 gallons (22.7 litres) of water – can be used in early autumn and the soil dug over in later autumn. The treated area can be used for normal sowing and planting in the spring *except for* beetroots or turnips. Once your plot is clear of weeds life becomes a little easier, for your crops themselves help to clear the soil, although the finer the tilth the easier it is for annual weeds to grow. Constant vigilance and a hoe always at the ready are the best answer.

Planning your plot

If you have an allotment your plot will almost certainly be symmetrical in shape. This may not be true of the garden plot, but in designing your plot some common points must be remembered. One is the need for a service area where you can have your toolshed or something more elaborate: also perhaps a greenhouse and a frame or two. Another is to provide access to the interior of your plot by paths along which you can wheel your wheelbarrow. And don't forget in laying out your beds that some of them (e.g. for soft fruits, asparagus, strawberries etc) will be permanent or semi-permanent. If you are lucky enough to have a fence or wall on the west, north or east sides then it is wise to have a good border bed where full advantage can be taken of the reflected warmth throughout the day. Don't forget your compost and a corner for your bonfire. When possible avoid planting tall-growing vegetables or fruit trees on the south side of your garden as they will cut out the sun. To take full advantage of the sun's rays your vegetable rows should run as nearly as possible from south to north.

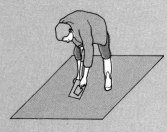

Keep your wooden mud scraper (see page 30) handy for cleaning spades. Near your shed is the place for a boot scraper.

Even if you cannot, at the start, achieve the standard of this design it will remind you of the principles on which it is based.

1 The fruit trees (which could be cordoned, espaliered or fanned) are planted on the north side to capture the sun and avoid shading other parts of the garden.

2 Possible site for a small herb garden, or the herbs could be distributed along the sunny border bed, possibly as border decoration. The border bed, especially with fence, wall or wattle, can be immensely useful for tomatoes and other crops, also catch crops such as radishes.

3 Large open beds suitable for main vegetable crops: potatoes, brassicas, peas, beans etc.

4 Seed bed close to working area, potting shed etc.

5 Bed for rhubarb, vegetable marrows & peas etc.

6 Strawberry bed.

7 Asparagus bed.

8 Hard-surface working area: a boot-scraper could be useful here.

9 Shed for storing wheelbarrow, tools, fertilisers, pots etc. If it is large enough, interior shelves are always useful.

10 Greenhouse on north side to get full benefit of sun, adjacent to seed bed.

11 Cold and/or hot frames for forcing early plants.

12 Compost heap or containers, preferably partly shaded.

13 Bonfire and incinerator site.

14 Water supply in working area if possible.

15 Paths providing easy access with wheelbarrow, tools etc to all parts of the garden.

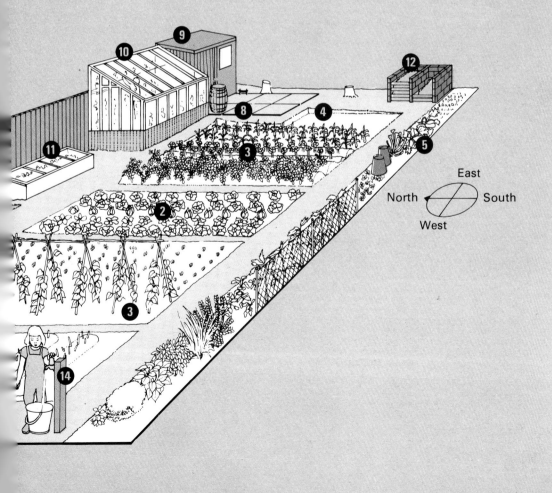

Down to earth

The best way to test the soil of your allotment is to pick up a good handful of moist (not wet) soil and squeeze it gently. You can learn a lot from this simple test.

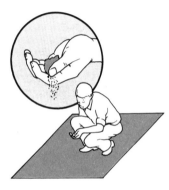

Your soil has its own particular features, so to get the best results from it you must be able to assess its qualities.

Some soil signals

If you have:

good leafy crops, the nitrogen content of your soil is OK;

good bean and pea crops, the potash content of your soil is OK;

flourishing rhododendrons or azaleas, there is an acid tendency.

Danger signals

Leaves scorched at the edges probably mean a potash deficiency.

Small plants with pale foliage probably mean a nitrogen deficiency.

Small plants with poor roots probably mean a phosphate deficiency.

Small plants, poor roots, and yellow leaves probably mean a calcium deficiency.

	Soil Characteristics	How to recognise
Sandy soil	Light. Dries out very quickly, badly needs watering in summer. Usually deficient in plant foods.	Feels gritty between the fingers and will not form a ball when rolled in the hand.
Clay soil	Very heavy to work. May get waterlogged in winter and crack in dry weather. Unsuitable for early crops as it is cold.	Resists changing shape when it is rolled between finger and thumb.
Loam	The gardener's friend, between sandy and clay without their disadvantages.	Dark and will form a ball when rolled in the hand, but soil separates when thumb presses ball.
Chalky soil	Poor soil for vegetables. Drains freely, sticky when wet.	The white chalky subsoil is usually there to see.
Peaty soil	Poor soil for growing but potentially very rich if treated properly.	Dark, sometimes black. Rich in organic matter, spongy to feel.

Lime

A most important ingredient of your soil is lime and as it is gradually washed out by rain it needs to be replaced. Too little lime means that the soil grows acid, destroying helpful bacteria and worms. Lime contains calcium (one of the essential plant foods), breaks up clay soil and discourages pests. Soil-testing outfits can be bought very cheaply and will show whether the lime content is up to the mark. They are easy to use but follow the instructions carefully, because too much lime can also cause trouble.

Autumn, before manuring, is the best time to apply the lime as a top-dressing to be worked in by the rain. Vegetable plots should be limed every three years, but avoid liming soil to be used for potatoes. The best way is to lime each year that section to be used for brassicas. With the rotation of crops this should mean the liming of the whole plot over three years.

Humus

Another vital ingredient of your soil is humus, partially decomposed organic matter that is in the process of being broken down by bacteria in the soil. It is important, therefore – particularly with free draining soils – to feed with humus makers. These can be either partly decomposed, e.g. compost (see pages 44–45) and well-rotted manure, or undecomposed, e.g. grass-cuttings, annual weeds or 'green manure'. Green manure is any cheap quick-growing crop grown specially for the purpose of digging into the soil, and is particularly useful with sandy or chalky soils.

Improving your soil

Sandy
Because of its nature it loses plant foods and water easily. Dig in plenty of organic material (manure, compost etc) and fertiliser in spring and autumn.

Clay
Look at your drainage first. Clay soil should be well broken up by autumn digging, lime added to help the process further and generous supplies of compost, manure etc dug in.

Loam
Not so much a question of improving as maintaining. The usual autumn digging and regular dressings of lime, fertilisers etc should keep up its virtues.

Chalky
As in sandy soil, the free drainage causes plant food to be washed away. Don't dig too deeply and add plenty of compost and/or manure with plenty of fertiliser too.

Peaty
Because it is rich in plant remains this soil can be dramatically improved by ensuring proper drainage, adding lime to remove acidity and digging in loam topsoil.

Manure

The days when small boys earned pennies from gardeners by following horse-drawn traffic with a bucket and spade are long since gone. But animal manure is still procurable in the country and near the growing number of riding stables. Animal manure should not be fed to the soil while fresh, but covered with some soil and allowed to rot. Dig in during the autumn, about 7 lb (3.2 kg) to the square yard.

Give us the tools

To misquote Churchill, 'give us the tools and we'll start the job.' Some tools are essential, others very useful, others almost in the luxury bracket. You can't start without a fork and spade: these come in various sizes and weights. Then, when your soil is dug you will need a draw hoe to help break up the small clods and a rake to level off and produce a fine tilth. By this time you will have realised, with weeds to be carted to compost or bonfire, that you will need a wheelbarrow. Soon you will be planting out so you'll need a hand trowel and perhaps a

1 Spade for digging; can have straight or hollow (traditional) hand-grip, whichever suits you best. Stainless steel spades are expensive, but don't rust and are easily kept clean.
2 Fork for breaking and turning over earth. See remarks on spade.
3 a Hoes. Draw hoe useful for breaking small clods, helping to produce a fine tilth and aerate the soil, and for making deepish seed drills; dutch hoe useful for cutting off weeds just below surface between rows **3b**.
4 Rake for producing flat surface to soil, removing stones, hoed weeds etc and producing tilth.
5a Hand trowel and fork **5b**. The trowel is the most used, for lifting young plants, thinning, transplanting.
6 Watering can. When buying think of the weight when full.
7 Wheelbarrow for transporting rubbish to compost or bonfire, moving tools, full pots, seed boxes, fertilisers etc.
8 Secateurs for pruning soft fruit etc.
9 Shears for trimming hedges, shrubs etc if you

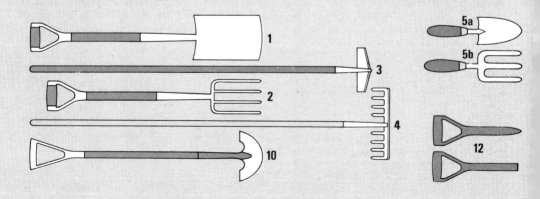

hand fork too, and if you have an old spade or fork handle make yourself a dibber by sharpening the end of the shaft. And you'll have discovered that you need a watering can to water your seedlings, and string for making straight rows, and labels to identify the rows. You may think you will remember what was sown where but you won't. You'll certainly find a use for shears, pruning knife and secateurs later. Always clean tools after use, and keep them indoors off the ground. Exposure to the weather rusts metal and rots wooden handles.

Best foot forward
It is advisable always to have a plank of wood handy in the working area. Laid down on the beds this enables the gardener to work when the soil is wet, without getting his boots muddy, and without stamping the soil down with deep footprints.

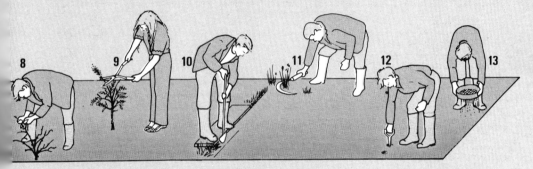

have them.
10 Edgecutter for making straight edges to the beds, a feature of a well-maintained vegetable plot. They can be achieved with a spade but more efficiently with a half-moon-shaped edger with a sharp cutting edge.
11 Sickle (or swat) for cutting down rough growth.
12 Dibbers for making a firm hole when planting such vegetables as brassicas, leeks etc.
13 Sieve for clearing stones from soil.
These lists of tools, essential or just useful, do not include the other articles you will inevitably acquire, such as pots, seed boxes, garden twine, a hose and perhaps a reel to keep it on.

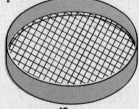

13

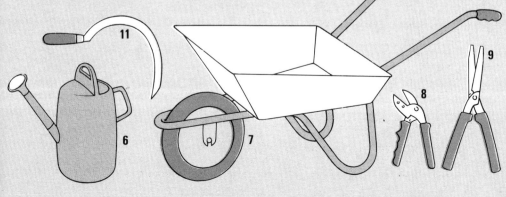

Storing your tools

Allotment sheds can range from slightly overgrown tool cupboards to the more splendid erections with windows and shelves, and roofs that fill your water butt, which, indeed, can be used almost as greenhouses. The two most important things demanding protection from the weather – in addition to the allotment holder, who may want to hop into the shed during a downpour – are his tools and his bags of perishable fertilisers, peat etc. Tools should be kept indoors because of the danger of rusting, and they are a temptation to thieves in the open. Chemicals and fertilisers need protection because, exposed to the elements, bags may split and the contents deteriorate. Take care to dispose of chemical containers according to instructions to prevent accidents.

Dig this
A useful rough device for cleaning spades can be made by the handyman. It is made of wood and resembles a cross between a miniature spade and a flat-bladed, wedged trowel. Very useful for peeling the mud off the real spade.

Whatever its size your shed is best with a solid floor of concrete, stone or brick to prevent it being churned into mud in winter and dust in summer. Whatever the size of your roof, fix a gutter and pipe to catch rain water: it's surprising how much runs off even a small roof. Have a lock, if only a padlock, on your door to deter the casual thief.

If you don't have a damp-proof floor, store tools off the floor on a low shelf or hung from hooks. A few shelves are invaluable for small articles as listed above and for chemicals, fertiliser bags etc. Keep a hook for your coat and a corner for boots, but remember to leave a corner where you can stand when the rain comes down.

In your shed, don't forget to take advantage of the roof. You can hang netting, coils of wire, canes, or a watering can from hooks, out of the way but easily reached.

Even if you are keeping fertilisers etc indoors it is wise to have them if possible in bags or containers that won't split: a heap of bonemeal on your shed floor is not going to do anyone any good. At appropriate times you can expect to have quite a few bags to house – peat, bonemeal, sulphate of lime, sulphate of potash etc – all of which take up room.

Apart from these it is surprising what a vast number of small articles need a home: your pegs and strings, seed labels, dibber, a ball of string or twine, a measuring stick, wire for the raspberries, a hone, canes, netting when out of use, perhaps some plastic sheeting, a watering can, syringe or sprayer, and packets of slug pellets are just a few of them. You will also want to keep old peat and fertiliser bags, but these fold up neatly.

Call a spade a spade, but a shovel a shovel. They are used for different purposes: the spade for digging, the shovel for scooping. The spade is driven into the ground and pressed in further with the foot. The shovel is used horizontally to the ground to lift a load from a pile or heap. Cunning shovellers use the right knee to help drive the shovel home.

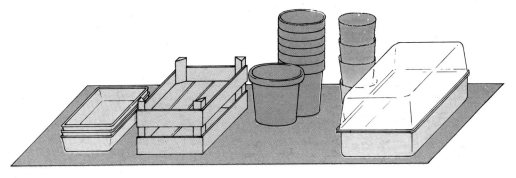

Seed boxes and pots *can* be kept outside but they are safer from the light-fingered inside; never leave fibrous pots – usually made of a peat mixture – outside as they will be rotted by rain. Plastic seed boxes are easiest to store, because they will usually fit one inside the other, whereas wooden boxes make bulky piles.

Pots can be made of clay, plastic or peat fibre. The latter present no storage problem except before use, because they are planted with the plant. All other pots, particularly the clay variety, should be scrubbed clean before storing. Clay pots should be thoroughly soaked before using.

Sent to try us

The allotment holder is by no means free of enemies (see also pages 110–113). They can be of the four-legged or two-legged variety and, alas, some of the latter may be humans. Chief among the four-legged varieties are mice, rats, rabbits (rabbit populations now on the increase again), cats and dogs which tend to scratch up your new seed rows. But don't forget that dogs chase off rabbits and cats keep off mice and birds, one of your two-legged enemies. And birds that eat

Rabbits Shooting them in an allotment area could be dangerous sport. If they are a real nuisance the only thing to do is to keep them out with wire netting around the boundary. Don't forget that rabbits are burrowing creatures so bury the lower part of your netting about 9 in (22 cm) below the soil level.

Birds Criss-crossed black thread tied to pegs and stretched over seedlings helps to deter birds. So do scaring devices such as flapping plastic bags tied to canes, or pieces of glittering foil blowing in the wind. But the most effective way to protect crops is to stretch nylon netting or wire crop guards over them.

Cats and Dogs There's really not very much you can do about these except to offer up thanks that they are carnivores and not vegetarians. Adequate fences and gates are something of a deterrent, especially if they are wired against rabbits, but even these can be jumped. You are not likely to get any damages from the animal's owner unless you can prove that he incited the dog or cat to scratch up your seed rows.

seedlings also eat insects that may attack your plants, so there is an element of compensation all round. The human variety of enemy, regrettably, is the thief and here there is rarely compensation. Tools can be locked away, but, unfortunately, the price of vegetables today makes a good crop a valuable haul. Safest is an allotment surrounded by others: for obvious reasons, those on the outskirts are most attractive to thieves.

Thieves and trespassers
There's not much you can do about thieves except keep a watchful eye on your property and hope that malefactors will be caught and suitably punished. As for trespass actual damage has to be proved in the civil courts by the allotment holder before he can get damages, which are likely to be nominal anyway.

Windbreaks Your allotment agreement will probably lay down that you have to keep hedges properly cut and trimmed and maintain fences and gates in repair. It will also probably require you not to cause any nuisance or annoyance to the occupiers of neighbouring allotments, so care should be exercised in erecting high windbreaks, sheds etc which might overshadow them.

Weeds Dig *in* annual weeds as green manure but not if they have flowered. Dig *out* perennials and burn them (see pages 22–23). Never allow dock or thistle to seed. Dig out couch grass (quitch) whenever you see it. Don't forget that if you allow weeds to get out of hand you can be compelled by the authorities to prevent them spreading.

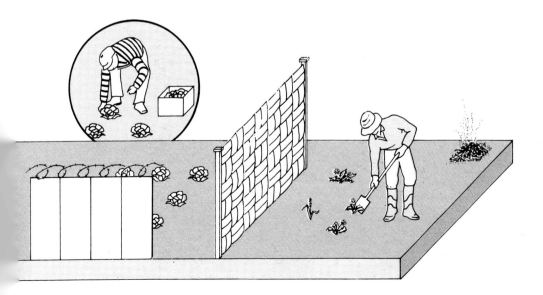

Trench warfare

If possible get digging done before winter to enable frost to break up the soil. There are two forms of digging, digging and double-digging, and the second is twice as laborious. In most plots double-digging is not necessary but it can help where deep-rooted vegetables are to grow or on badly drained heavy land. With digging, the soil is dug one spit (spade blade) deep: in double-digging, after digging one spit down, the subsoil is forked over. In both cases the principle is to keep the fertile topsoil on top.

In trenching, trench 1 is dug out and the topsoil removed to the other end of the section. Compost or manure is laid along the trench. Trench 2 is then dug out and its topsoil turned over into trench 1 (grass and annual weeds can remain at the bottom of the trench to rot but perennials should be pulled out). Topsoil from trench 3 goes into trench 2 and so on until soil from trench 1 goes into the last trench.

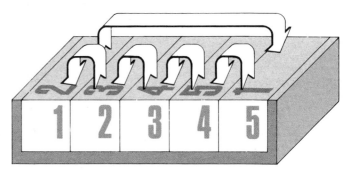

When digging, mark your first trench one spit wide. Drive the spade in one spit deep at right angles to the sides, then along the trench marks. Remove the squares of soil to the other end of the section to be dug. In later trenches turn the squares over before tipping them into the trench just dug out. A compromise with double-digging is to drive the spade at intervals into the subsoil.

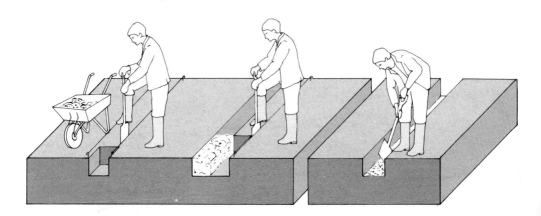

Paths If you rent your allotment you will probably not want to lay permanent paths. In that case you must be satisfied with trodden earth or grass. Both have disadvantages: the former, in bad weather, can be dirty and slippery; the latter require the edges to be trimmed, and couch grass should never be allowed to establish itself, as it will spread. For more permanent paths dig a shallow trench and lay a solid foundation, well tamped down, of rubble or clinker before putting the surface down. If this is to be of bricks or stones, lay a basis of mortar on the foundation into which the bricks or stone can be pressed.

Straight edges to beds and paths make all the difference to the appearance of your allotment. A nice straight edge with a slight trough where soil is thrown back on the bed looks neat, but the trough tends to fill up as it weathers. A thin board driven down between bed and path, especially if the latter is clinker or ashes, keeps things neat but it is not cheap.

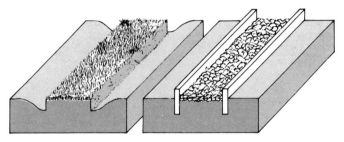

With double-digging, practice is the same as with digging except that before the topsoil is turned in, the heavy subsoil at the bottom of the trench is well forked over. In both digging and double-digging the spade should be driven down into the ground as straight as possible.

When you are digging from scratch, find out what your soil is like. It's important because it is a guide to what you can grow successfully, and to what deficiencies you may have to make up. Soils range from stony to clay through peat, chalk, sand and loam.

Stony soil is hard to cultivate because it drains quickly and dries out; clay is inclined to get waterlogged and is not good for early crops. The best soil is a medium loam. By drainage and the use of manures and fertilisers, composts and lime, the character of soil can be improved.

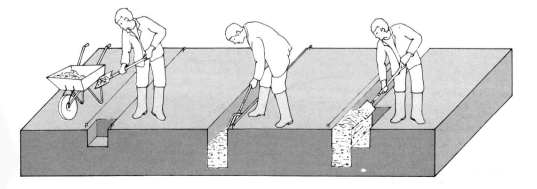

Under glass

Growing 'under glass' may mean many things. Some plants, e.g. tomatoes, may spend their whole lives in the greenhouse. Others spend only their infancy under glass, in frames or greenhouses. Others may be forced in the allotment under cloches. The whole purpose of growing under glass is to produce conditions that are milder and more controllable than the natural conditions and therefore more conducive to rapid growth. Seedlings grown in this way tend to be delicate and before they are planted out should undergo a hardening-off period to prepare them for the more rigorous conditions outside.

Basic greenhouse features

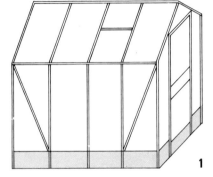

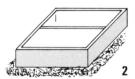

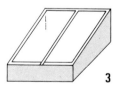

Aristocrat of the 'under glass' family is the greenhouse (1), dealt with on pages 40–41. If you are lucky enough to have a greenhouse you will be able to work inside it in comfort in bad weather and to grow plants more scientifically, for temperature, light and ventilation and to some extent soil can be controlled. Most greenhouses have one or two natural soil beds and staging or shelving provides space for pots and seed boxes in which to prepare seedlings for their outside life. The main purpose of forcing is to have seedlings ready to plant out when otherwise, because of the weather, you would only be able to sow seeds. Cloches (4)–(5) see pages 38–39 – have the great advantage of being portable and can be moved from crop to crop. In cold frames (3) and greenhouses it is best to grow in pots or seed boxes: in hot frames (2) the soil temperature plays the important part, so sow direct in the soil. Although the whole idea of a greenhouse is to capture the rays of the sun and protect plants from the wind it is important to shade the house from too much sun.

Hot frame

If you are lucky enough to obtain some fresh strawy manure in November or December you may well consider making a hot frame. This is half way between a cold frame and a heated greenhouse and is cost free to run as it uses the natural heat engendered by the fermentation of the manure. Mark out the area required, i.e. about 18 in (45 cm) longer and wider than the frame itself. Dig this marked area to a depth of 6 in (15 cm) and fill the hole with layers of the manure mixed with leaves. Previously the manure and leaves should have been turned over at weekly intervals and watered if dry. The manure should be built up to about 21 in (52 cm) in height, i.e. 15 in (37 cm) above soil level, and trodden down lightly. The frame is then placed centrally on the hot bed leaving an overlap around it (this helps to control the temperature). Inside the frame put 4–5 in (10–12 cm) of light soil mixed with peat. Put the glass on and you have your hot frame. Do not sow anything for about a week, as at first when the frame is closed considerable heat is generated. Soil temperatures should be a little over 80°F (27°C) before sowing.

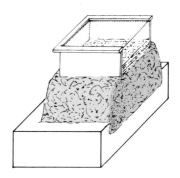

The hot frame is not just a useful method of growing seedlings and bringing on bedding-out plants. Its main purpose is to bring suitable crops to complete but early maturity. Both jobs can be done at the same time. Lettuce seed, for example, can be sown between rows of maturing lettuces, or in boxes, but must be pricked out fairly soon.

Cold frame
'Cold' frames is really a misnomer. Their purpose is simply to provide a warmer atmosphere without artificial heat (although this can be used too). The sides protect the inside from the cold wind and the sloping glass top ('light') takes full advantage of the heat of the sun. So site your cold frame in a spot protected from the wind but exposed to the sun. It is inadvisable to use garden soil in the cold frame, because it contains the seeds of weeds. Best to use is a seed sowing compost such as John Innes. Early lettuces can be sown as early as February or as late as November. Fill a seed tray with compost up to about ½ in (1 cm) from the top. Level the surface, then scatter seeds and sieve a shallow layer of compost over them. Don't be too generous with the seed as overcrowded seedlings tend to suffocate and are hard to transplant. Pelleted seeds can be sown well-spaced and pricking out thus avoided; the soil must be kept reasonably moist or the seed coating will not dissolve. Never forget that while your cold frame protects seeds and plants from wind it also keeps out the rain, so watering needs to be maintained.

For a cheap forcing frame, persuade your greengrocer or grocer to give you a wooden fruit box. Remove the bottom and place the sides on the prepared soil. Cover the top of the box with glass or polythene and you can then use it to bring on your seedlings.

Cloches

In the early part of the year cloches take full advantage of weak sunshine and protect plants from late frosts: in the latter part they protect them from frost and bleak winds. The simplest cloche is the jamjar but because of its size its use is limited to small seedlings. The older type of cloche was bell-shaped, and useful for individual plants; today's are shaped like miniature greenhouses or hangars, and placed next to each other they can cover a whole row. But take care not to create a tunnel for cold winds to blow along. Watch out for sharp edges on glass cloches.

You need not wait to sow your seeds or for your plants to be ready for bedding out before putting your cloches out. This can be done two or three weeks ahead, so that the soil, partly protected from frost and rain, becomes warmer and provides favourable conditions for growth.

Cloches are usually made of glass or plastic, sometimes reinforced with wire. Some examples are shown here. The plastic varieties are cheaper and lighter but require to be anchored from the wind.

The timetable below shows when you can sow under cloches. As the weather becomes warmer the cloches can be removed. Always water seed rows before putting cloches over them. Unless the weather is very dry not much later watering is required, as moisture condensing inside the cloches and penetration from surrounding soil usually keeps the plants happy.

Cover up story
If you have no cloches, don't forget the humble jamjar. It can serve the same purpose for a while, bringing on seedlings and protecting them from frost.

If you are lucky enough to have a window in your shed, have a shelf under it so that you can use it to hold a seed tray or two in which to bring on seedlings – every little helps.

Cloches timetable
1 January, fork over ground. **2** Firm down. **3** Rake for tilth. **4** Put out cloches to warm the soil (seal ends). **5** Sow seeds (see timetable opposite). **6** Weeds will continue to grow under cloches and will flourish if uncontrolled. Seedlings also need to be thinned out so cloches have to be lifted from time to time for weeding and thinning. When cloches are not being used they should be cleaned and stored tidily.

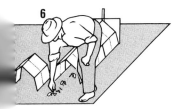

	Sow	
January	Broad beans	Lettuce
	Summer	Peas
	cauliflower	
February	Broad beans	Lettuce
	Summer cabbage	Peas
	Carrots	Radishes
	Summer	Summer spinach
	cauliflower	Turnips
March	Summer cabbage	
	Carrots	
	Harvest	
April	Radishes	Carrots
	Summer spinach	Lettuce
May	Carrots	
	Summer	Peas
	cauliflower	Summer spinach
	Lettuce	Turnips
June	Peas	
	Broad beans	Summer
	Summer cabbage	cauliflower
	Carrots	Turnips
July	Broad beans	
	Summer cabbage	

Autumn and winter: use cloches to shelter Parsley, Seakale, Spinach, French beans etc.

Greenhouses

It is possible to run a flourishing allotment or vegetable garden without a greenhouse, but any gardener who does have one knows the tremendous advantages it confers. There are many types of greenhouses: of glass, plastic, even fibreglass; with aluminium or timber frames; and freestanding or lean-to. But the principle is the same with all of them: to ensure protected conditions more favourable to growth than those prevailing outside. In such conditions plants should grow 'according to the book' and not be subject to weather, frost, excessive wet, or some garden pests. Different plants demand different conditions and the thing to do is to maintain the average condition in which they can all flourish.

Whether or not you heat a greenhouse it will provide shelter and some warmth, although the contribution it makes is obviously enhanced if you do heat it. On an allotment you are unlikely to have electricity laid on, but simpler methods such as paraffin or gas heaters are comparatively inexpensive to run, and by using polythene you can make a primitive form of double glazing. A thermometer is important, but don't forget that it is not just a question of temperature but of humidity too. Paraffin or gas heaters cause problems with humidity. Care must be taken to maintain moisture levels and correct temperature.

The freestanding span-roof greenhouse (1) has the advantage that it can be sited anywhere in the allotment or garden. The three-quarter span and the lean-to (2) both require a wall against which they are erected. The three-quarter span, as can be seen, provides higher roof space.

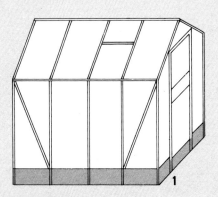

1

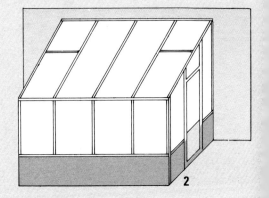

2

1 To take full advantage of the greenhouse, plan your staging carefully in accordance with its size. The lowest shelf, apart from housing pots, seed boxes etc should provide a useful working surface. Shelving is ranged to take full advantage of the sun.

2 Ventilation is important in winter and summer. In winter it is needed to control the humidity produced by artificial heat: an overheated greenhouse in summer is as dangerous as an unheated one in winter.

3 Indeed it may well be necessary to shade your plants from excessive heat by using blinds outside the house.

4 It is important to have at least a stone or concrete path down the centre of the house or along by the staging. Plants can be grown, of course, under the first shelf at floor level.

Where it is desired to germinate a few seeds rapidly a propagator box is useful. It can be used in the home, where there is an electricity supply, and the seedlings later moved to the greenhouse. There are several varieties of propagator but they all work on the same principle. One of the simplest is a fairly deep plastic tray onto which fits an ordinary plastic seed tray. In the lower tray is fitted a low-power electric bulb – 25 watts provides enough heat. The seeds, in small peat pots, are placed in the upper tray, which is covered with polythene. In the heat thus generated, seeds will germinate quickly even in in January.

Freestanding greenhouses are best sited with the longer sides facing north and south. Foundations vary: the greenhouse can be placed on a low brick wall or on concrete footings. It is advisable to have a solid stone or concrete pathway running down the centre, leaving soil beds on either side if desired.

Basic features of a greenhouse

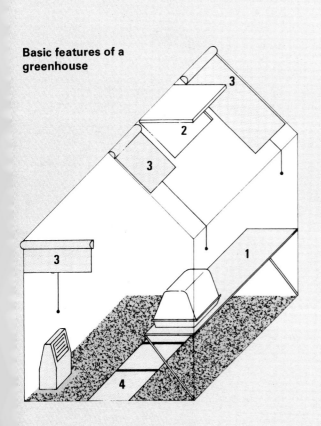

Feeding your plot

All gardens or allotments need feeding with fertilisers at some time. These can be applied as top-dressing, i.e. they are scattered on the surface, or as base-dressing, i.e. they are dug into the soil before planting to help feed the roots as they grow. Some fertilisers (foliar feed) can be sprayed on the leaves of growing plants. Fertilisers are divided into organic and inorganic ones. The former come from animals or plants, the latter are manufactured chemically: both have their virtues. Well-rotted manure is easily the best of the lot but is no longer easy to obtain. Plants need three major foods, nitrogen, phosphates and potash; also calcium and a number of what are called trace elements, i.e. tiny quantities of such minerals as iron, sulphur and manganese. Fertilisers can maintain the supply of the three major foods; to ensure the calcium you must provide lime; and the addition of humus should ensure that the

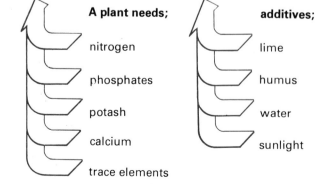

A plant needs;

nitrogen

phosphates

potash

calcium

trace elements

additives;

lime

humus

water

sunlight

Base-dressings (see next page) are usually dug in during autumn and winter so that the soil is enriched before sowing and planting take place. Remember that root crops tend to dislike recently manured ground, which may make the roots fork.

trace elements are there. Nitrogen stimulates growth and helps leaf formation; phosphates develop roots and leaves, and help plants to mature; and potash develops strong roots.

■ Fast
□ Slow
O = Organic
I = Inorganic

Each dressing contains one or more of the three major foods

Top-dressings:
■ Dried blood (O)
■ Fish meal (O)
□ Poultry manure (O)
■ Wood ash (O)
□ Nitro chalk (I)
■ Sulphate of ammonia (I)
■ Sulphate of potash (I)
■ Superphosphate of lime (I)

Base-dressings:
□ Bone meal (O)
□ Farmyard manure (O)
■ Hoof and horn (O)
□ Seaweed (O)
□ Hop manure (O)

Most top-dressings are needed in spring and summer, i.e. during the growing period. The fertiliser is worked in by hoeing and raking, and by rain and weather. Try not to scatter fertiliser on the leaves. Liquid fertiliser acts more quickly than dry.

Foliar feeds can be used to give plants a quick boost, especially if any show signs of being retarded. The feed is sprayed directly on the foliage and is rapidly absorbed and converted into plant food. The feed is made up of the three major plant foods plus the trace elements, all in the right proportion.

Home brew
If you have a water butt or old tank fed with rainwater from your shed roof and can get hold of some farmyard manure, make your own liquid manure. All you need do is put the manure in a small sack, tie the neck and suspend the sack in the butt.

Back to the land – compost

Well-made compost can be equal in value to farmyard manure. In most places the latter is hard to come by, whereas the materials to make compost are close at hand. Compost is basically decomposed vegetable matter and when returned to the soil it provides humus. The cheapest way of making it is in the traditional compost heap but simple containers, which are tidier, can be bought or you can make your own bin if you have bricks or boards or some wire netting handy. When making compost be sure

A good compost heap consists of a pile of sandwiches each made of about 6 in (15 cm) of mixed vegetable matter (**a**), covered by a thin layer of accelerator (**b**), covered by about 1 in (2.5 cm) of soil (**c**). The vegetable layer allows for aeration. Compost should be ready for use in two to three months in warm weather, or a month longer in cold weather.

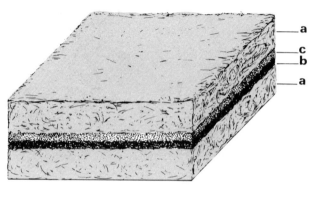

A useful bin that can be bought is this cylindrical plastic bin, the panels of which are raised so that the compost can be withdrawn from the bottom. The ingredients of the compost are the same as above. Bins are tidier than heaps.

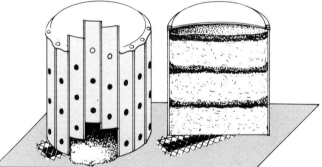

A home-made bin can be made with bricks, boards or wire netting. Whichever way it is made, it should have some elementary drainage such as a layer of broken bricks or stones. If bricks or boards are used for the bin they should be put together so as to allow for air penetration.

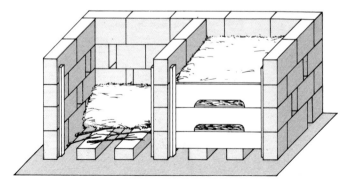

To make a compost heap, dig out a pit about 3 ft (1 m) square and about 6 in (15 cm) deep. Keep the soil handy for use as the heap grows. Fill the bottom of the pit with stones and bricks mixed with broken branches, cabbage stalks etc. This provides drainage as for home-made bins.

not to include vegetation from diseased plants or those that have flowered, or grass-cuttings after weedkiller has been used on the lawn, or twigs or woody stems. But you can use household refuse such as peelings, trimmed vegetable leaves, fruit skins and even eggshells. Grass-cuttings *alone* compress the heap and retard decomposition. Compost-making can be speeded up by using a proprietary accelerator or activator. Compost heaps should be about 3 ft (1 m) square and 3 ft (1 m) in height and as cube-shaped, rather than conical, as you can make them. To be ready for use the compost should be dark-coloured and crumbly, when it can be either dug in or spread on the surface and raked in for shallow-rooting crops.

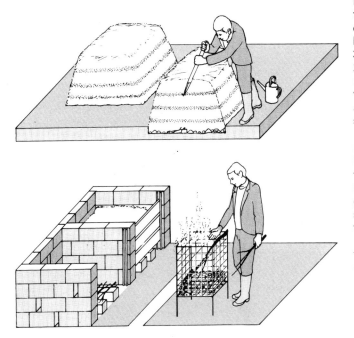

Then start building your heap as described opposite, making sure each layer is firmed down. The process continues over the weeks but when the heap is about 3 ft (1 m) high cover it with 2 in (5 cm) of soil and leave nature to take its course. As you build, keep it as cubic as you can. If the heap seems to have dried out, make holes with a stake and pour in water.

Do not use diseased plants, flowered plants, hedge-cuttings (except soft green clippings), brassica stalks, perennial weeds, tough stems, or remains of meat or fish. The place for these is the bonfire or the dustbin and the sooner they get there the better. Don't leave discarded vegetation around as a haven for slugs and snails.

Chapter two
Growing plans

Careful preparation always pays off when the autumn harvest grows to its full abundant splendour

So you are all prepared. You've got your tools, the soil is dug with a fine tilth, you've even polished the glass of your greenhouse, if you have one. Your packets of seeds are waiting to be opened. You want to see something growing but you are worried about when and how to sow, when you are likely to harvest, and how much.

Vegetables grow well mainly because they are sown or planted in the right way in the right place at the right time. As with humans the future health of the plant is determined by the handling it receives during infancy as much as by the loving care it gets later. Not for nothing are the beds for seedlings called nursery beds, and those who grow young plants called nurserymen.

That's what this chapter is about. It tells you why you should not lose heart if some seeds take longer to make a showing than others: You can check on the germination period of most common vegetables. You may be surprised to learn that from one tiny brussels sprout seed that has germinated you may eventually pick as much as 2 lb (0.9 kg) of sprouts. There is a table showing the sort of yield you can expect from every common vegetable. And there's another section explaining the need for the rotation of crops and how to organise it.

Did you know that many of the seeds left in the packet after you have sown your rows, which so many people throw away, are good for sowing not only next year but even longer? You can check how long each kind of seed keeps in this chapter.

A subsequent chapter tells you precisely how to sow, plant out and cultivate individual vegetables. This one explains the general rules. If you are a beginner they will help you to keep a sense of proportion, to understand the inexorable but often seemingly slow passage of the seasons, to expect modestly even if you hope extravagantly. Many failures would have been avoided had others followed these simple rules.

Planning the year No.1

This sowing calendar illustrates graphically the gardening cycle. The winter months are used for the heavy work of digging, manuring and generally preparing for the major growing period of the year. In February a few tough seeds may be sown in the open; then, as spring comes, the list of vegetables that can be sown grows, reaching its peak in April. Some vegetables appear in more than one month, because you can sow them in these months or they are sown for succession crops. After April sowing diminishes but the planting-out of seedlings grown under glass or bought from the nurseryman takes its place.

jan

You probably won't have completed winter work in the allotment by Christmas so take advantage of fine days in January to dig, manure and tidy up generally. Begin buying your seeds and start chitting early seed potatoes (see potatoes, pages 80–81). Start a new compost heap with rubbish as most will have been dug in. To clear as much ground as possible harvest those remaining crops that will store.

feb

Sow
Jerusalem artichokes
Garlic
Horseradish
Parsnips
Early peas
Early potatoes
Shallots

Just sow
Always read the instructions on seed packets. Yours may be a variety calling for special treatment.

mar

Sow
Broad beans
Brussels sprouts
Summer cabbage
Carrots
Autumn cauliflower
Winter cauliflower
Leeks
Lettuce
Onions
Parsnips
Peas
Potatoes
Radishes
Seakale
Shallots
Summer spinach
Turnips
Plant out
Asparagus
Red cabbage

You will probably have done your planning during the winter months and to some extent where you sow or plant out is already determined by your plan for rotating the crops (see pages 54–55), but the lists below show how sowing has to be fitted in. Many vegetables grow best where manuring or composting has been done some months before sowing and has been well dug in, or where there has been manuring for a previous crop. Don't forget to guard against pests by dusting seed and seedling rows with an appropriate insecticide, and protect seedlings with slug pellets.

may

Sow
Broad beans
French beans
Runner beans
Beetroot
Broccoli
Brussels sprouts
Autumn cabbage
Savoy cabbage
Summer cabbage
Carrots
Cauliflower
Kale
Leeks
Lettuce
Parsnips
Peas
Potatoes
Radishes
Perpetual spinach
Summer spinach
Turnips
Plant out
Asparagus

jun

Sow
French beans
Runner beans
Beetroot
Broccoli
Autumn cabbage
Winter cabbage
Carrots
Kale
Lettuce
Peas
Potatoes
Plant out
Brussels sprouts
Summer cabbage
Cauliflower
Cucumber
Green peppers
Sweet corn
Tomatoes

Sow
French beans
Runner beans
Beetroot
Chinese cabbage
Carrots
Chicory
Endive
Lettuce
Peas
Radishes
Spinach
Turnips
Plant out
Broccoli
Brussels sprouts
Cabbage
Cauliflower
Celeriac
Celery
Courgettes Marrows
Cucumber
Green peppers
Kale
Leeks
Sweet corn
Tomatoes

Planning the year No.2

Your planning will depend on two important factors: the space available, and whether you have frames or a greenhouse in which you can bring on seedlings more speedily. You may also want to consider the economics of buying seedlings at planting-out time from a reputable nurseryman. Growing from seed is cheaper but it needs both space and time, and if only small quantities are required (e.g. a dozen tomato plants) or if seedlings are cheap (e.g. leeks) it may pay you to buy. Sowing in seed boxes, pots or propagators under glass is not difficult but caring for seedlings is time-consuming.

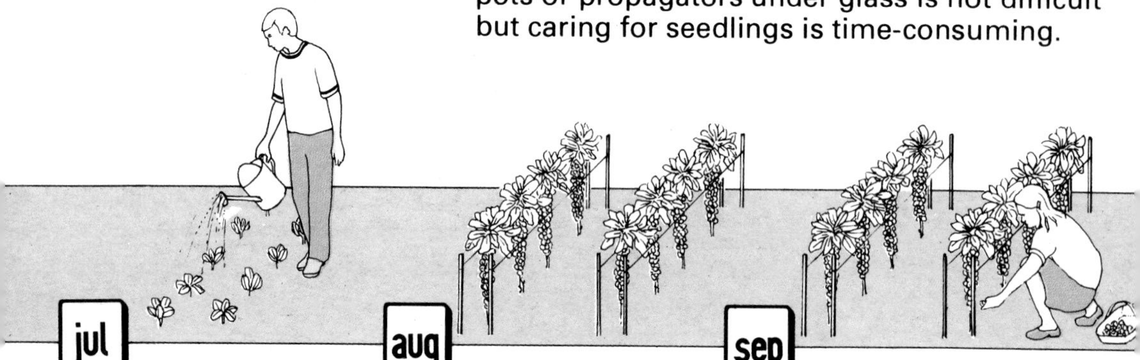

jul

Sow
French beans
Chinese cabbage
Spring cabbage
Carrots
Endive
Lettuce
Peas
Radishes
Spinach
Turnips
Plant out
Broccoli
Autumn cabbage
Savoy cabbage
Kale
Leeks

aug

Sow
Spring cabbage
Endive
Lettuce
Radishes
Perpetual spinach
Winter spinach
Turnips
Plant out
Savoy cabbage

sep

Sow
Red cabbage
Winter spinach
Plant out
Spring cabbage

On your marks
Fast-cropping plants (such as radishes and lettuces) can be used to mark seed rows of slower-growing plants (such as parsnips) if you sow both seeds in the same row at the same time.

Don't forget that some plants need a lot of space, whereas others require only a little; and that some mature quickly and others slowly. You can economise on space by sowing catch crops such as lettuce or radish, which mature quickly, alongside slower-growing vegetables. The radishes and lettuces will have been pulled and eaten long before the others are ripe for harvesting. Similarly you can sow early peas among early potatoes.

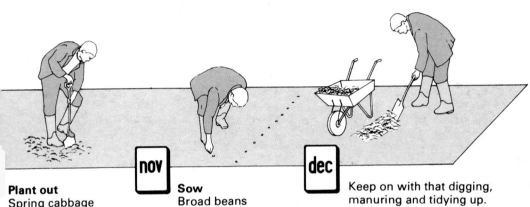

nov

dec

Plant out
Spring cabbage
No sowing. Get out the spade and start digging.

Sow
Broad beans
Next spring is getting nearer so keep on digging. You can start eating sprouts and lifting celery.

Keep on with that digging, manuring and tidying up. You may not be able to sow but you are helping to make sowing possible.

Eyes right
Don't worry if your seed potatoes vary in size and seemingly in quality; it doesn't matter. Little is good – sometimes better than big.

Keeping your distance

Vegetables are sown, thinned out or planted out at certain distances mainly because of the size to which they grow and the demands they make on the soil. Some are sown in seed beds, others in rows where they are to grow. Seedlings can be dibbled in – i.e. put in a hole made by a dibber – or planted in a hole made with a trowel. It is useful to have handy on the allotment a rod marked out up to 3 ft (1 m) for easy measurement.

Rows are usually marked out with the help of pegs and string but an ingenious method is to place the prongs of your rake along the edge of the bed so that the long handle rests on the soil. Gentle pressure on the handle makes a straight groove at right angles to the edge. Round seeds will roll neatly down to the bottom.

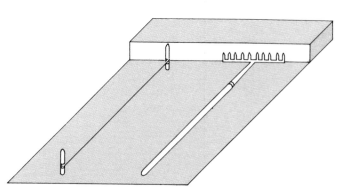

As the table opposite shows, seeds are sown in drills of different depths depending on the vegetable concerned. Many are sown in shallow drills only ½ or 1 in (1 or 2 cm) deep (**1** and **2**), larger seeds such as beans in deeper drills of 2 in (5 cm) (**3**) and sometimes it is useful to have a wide drill (**4**) so that more than one row can be sown or planted at a time.

Drills 1 and 2 can be made by drawing the corner of a hoe blade (**5**) lightly alongside a marking string. To make the deeper drill 3 the hoe blade is pressed deeper into the soil (**6**). The flat shallow trench-like drill 4 can be made by using a spade horizontally (**7**). Seeds are not always sown in rows but sometimes are scattered broadcast. To do this (**8**), pour some seeds into the open palm and then rap the hand smartly with the forefinger of the other hand, moving the extended palm over the sowing area. Large seeds are often sown in threes (**9**): when the seedlings grow the two weakest are thinned out.

After seeds have been placed in the drill, the dislodged earth, which should be very fine, is replaced, and sowing is not complete until the soil has been firmed down. Don't forget the labels.

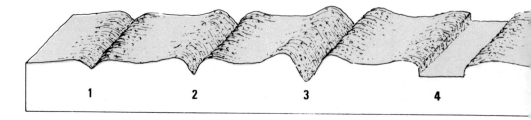

1   2   3   4

Column **A** shows the growing distance between plants, i.e. after thinning
Column **B** shows the distance between rows
Column **C** shows the depth of planting or sowing

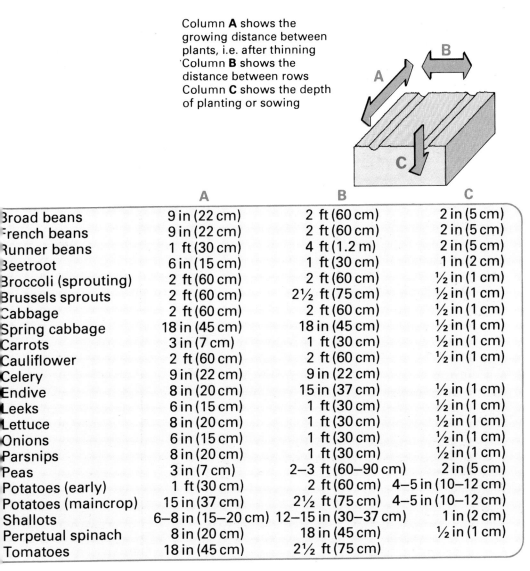

	A	B	C
Broad beans	9 in (22 cm)	2 ft (60 cm)	2 in (5 cm)
French beans	9 in (22 cm)	2 ft (60 cm)	2 in (5 cm)
Runner beans	1 ft (30 cm)	4 ft (1.2 m)	2 in (5 cm)
Beetroot	6 in (15 cm)	1 ft (30 cm)	1 in (2 cm)
Broccoli (sprouting)	2 ft (60 cm)	2 ft (60 cm)	½ in (1 cm)
Brussels sprouts	2 ft (60 cm)	2½ ft (75 cm)	½ in (1 cm)
Cabbage	2 ft (60 cm)	2 ft (60 cm)	½ in (1 cm)
Spring cabbage	18 in (45 cm)	18 in (45 cm)	½ in (1 cm)
Carrots	3 in (7 cm)	1 ft (30 cm)	½ in (1 cm)
Cauliflower	2 ft (60 cm)	2 ft (60 cm)	½ in (1 cm)
Celery	9 in (22 cm)	9 in (22 cm)	
Endive	8 in (20 cm)	15 in (37 cm)	½ in (1 cm)
Leeks	6 in (15 cm)	1 ft (30 cm)	½ in (1 cm)
Lettuce	8 in (20 cm)	1 ft (30 cm)	½ in (1 cm)
Onions	6 in (15 cm)	1 ft (30 cm)	½ in (1 cm)
Parsnips	8 in (20 cm)	1 ft (30 cm)	½ in (1 cm)
Peas	3 in (7 cm)	2–3 ft (60–90 cm)	2 in (5 cm)
Potatoes (early)	1 ft (30 cm)	2 ft (60 cm)	4–5 in (10–12 cm)
Potatoes (maincrop)	15 in (37 cm)	2½ ft (75 cm)	4–5 in (10–12 cm)
Shallots	6–8 in (15–20 cm)	12–15 in (30–37 cm)	1 in (2 cm)
Perpetual spinach	8 in (20 cm)	18 in (45 cm)	½ in (1 cm)
Tomatoes	18 in (45 cm)	2½ ft (75 cm)	

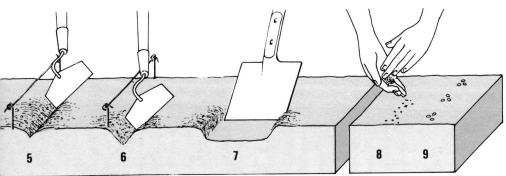

The rotation of crops

'The rotation of crops' sounds like something very grand in agriculture but it applies also to simple allotments and vegetable gardens. Different vegetables make different demands on the soil. Some, such as peas and beans, leave nitrogen in the soil, whereas brassicas, for example, like nitrogen very much. So it is sensible to grow brassicas in soil where, last year, you grew peas and beans. Likewise some crops do not like recent manuring, but last year's manuring can suit them very well.

In Year One, a typical layout of your allotment may include peas and beans, spinach and celery (1–4), root crops (5–8) and brassicas (9–12).

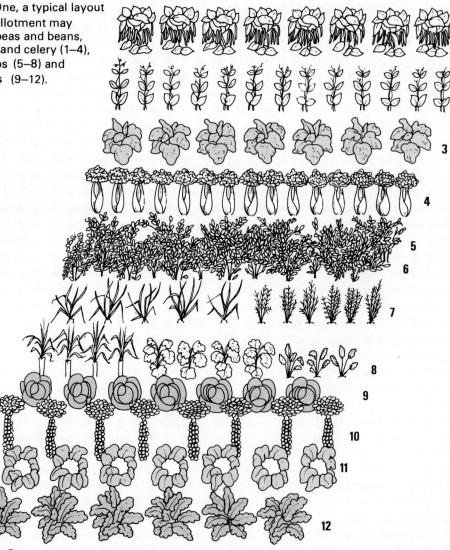

Year One

A three-year plan

In planning your rotation think of a three-year period and divide your plot roughly into three sections (see below). In sections 1 to 4 of Year One you can aim to grow the legumes (peas and beans), and perhaps spinach, celery etc. In between the peas and beans you can intercrop such quick-growing catch crops as lettuces and radishes. Sections 5 to 8 of Year One would be taken up by root crops, probably mostly potatoes, but also carrots, onions, turnips, parsnips and leeks. Potatoes break up the ground and help clear it, so they leave a patch in good heart for next year's peas, beans etc. Sections 9 to 12 in Year One could be devoted to the brassicas, providing you with your winter greens. So the practice of rotation is quite simple; but don't feel that you have to stick to the pattern too rigidly. Rotation is also a protection against the pests or diseases that may strike one of your crops. These often remain in the soil and if the same vegetable is grown in the same soil the following year the pest or disease will strike again. With a three-year rotation plan two years elapse before the same crop returns to the infected soil, which by then, it is hoped, will be clean.

In Year Two, you could then grow the brassicas where the legumes had been, the legumes on the site of your root crops, and the root crops where the brassicas were in Year One. In Year Three, move them all round again, so that the root crops would be where the brassicas grew in Year Two, the brassicas where the Year Two legumes were, and the legumes on the ground where the root crops grew in Year Two.

1 Beans
2 Peas
3 Spinach
4 Celery
5 Potatoes
6 Potatoes
7 Onions, carrots
8 Leeks, turnips, parsnips
9 Cabbages
10 Brussels sprouts
11 Cauliflower
12 Broccoli

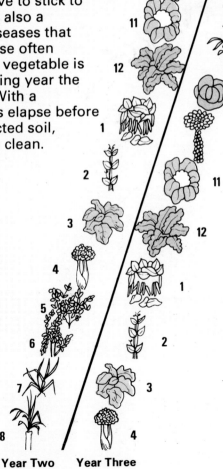

Year Two   Year Three

Sowing in the open

There are different ways of sowing. It can be done in boxes or in pots or direct in the allotment beds. Seed can be sown broadcast or in drills. With large and pelleted seeds no thinning out may be required, although it pays to sow two or three at each growing point, later thinning out to leave only the strongest seedling. Remember in bedding out that the tenderest and most vulnerable part of the seedling is not the leaf, as you might think, but the stem; so it is advisable to handle seedlings by the leaves.

Sowing in trays or pots
1 Clean before use.
2 Make sure pots are properly drained by putting broken crocks over hole, trays by putting roughage over slits.
3 Fill with seed compost to ½ in (1 cm) from top.
4 Firm down and level off.
5 Water lightly.
6 Sow small seed broadcast by emptying seed into palm and tapping outstretched hand.

7 Cover with thin layer of sieved compost. Water lightly with fine spray and keep moist.
8 When seedlings are large enough to handle, space them out in another box or tray filled with potting compost, about 40 to the box. Lift with a small piece of wood and firm in well. Keep compost moist until seedlings are large enough to bed out.

Keeping pot plants moist
Put pot in a larger one and pack moist peat around it.

The soil where your seedlings are finally to grow will have been well prepared and raked to a fine tilth. Mark out, with a cane pressed into the soil or a piece of stretched string, where your rows are to run. You will probably use a trowel to plant your seedlings or a dibber for long-rooted vegetables such as brassicas. Firm down the soil around the seedlings, dust the row with an appropriate insecticide for future protection and scatter slug pellets for immediate protection. Water the seedlings and step back and admire your handiwork.

Don't hang around when planting out. The seedling is bound to suffer shock from being lifted from the only home it has ever known and being transferred to strange and different surroundings. It is really uprooted. The quicker the transfer takes place the better. Try not to damage the roots in any way; one method of avoiding this is to keep as much soil as possible round them when you lift the seedling (**9**). But when bedding out pot-grown plants, loosen the roots gently and spread them out (**10**). Always water in, and plant out on a day when the soil is moist. The top of the soil ball should be just below soil level. If you have grown your seedlings in peat pots, you need not remove them (**11**). Just water well and put pot and all in a hole, with the rim just below soil level (**12**).

Taking root

Few moments are more gratifying to the gardener than when he sees the thin green line which shows that the seeds he sowed have germinated. There is still much to do, but now he really has something to work on. It may be a fairly long wait, for some plants take a long time to germinate. Others germinate very quickly, and these are useful as catch crops: among them are lettuces and radishes. Brassicas take longer, and potatoes and carrots are longer still. Parsley is one of the slowest to germinate. The diagram below shows the comparative germination periods of different groups of common vegetables and approximately when you can expect to harvest the fruits of your labours. The maturing period varies with the varieties grown. For example, early potatoes can mature in about 90 days but maincrop take much longer. Similarly, late varieties of brassicas etc take longer to mature than earlies. In general, vegetables that germinate quickly also mature comparatively quickly. It is important to remember that many crops may well be harvested before they are completely mature and this means cropping over a longer period.

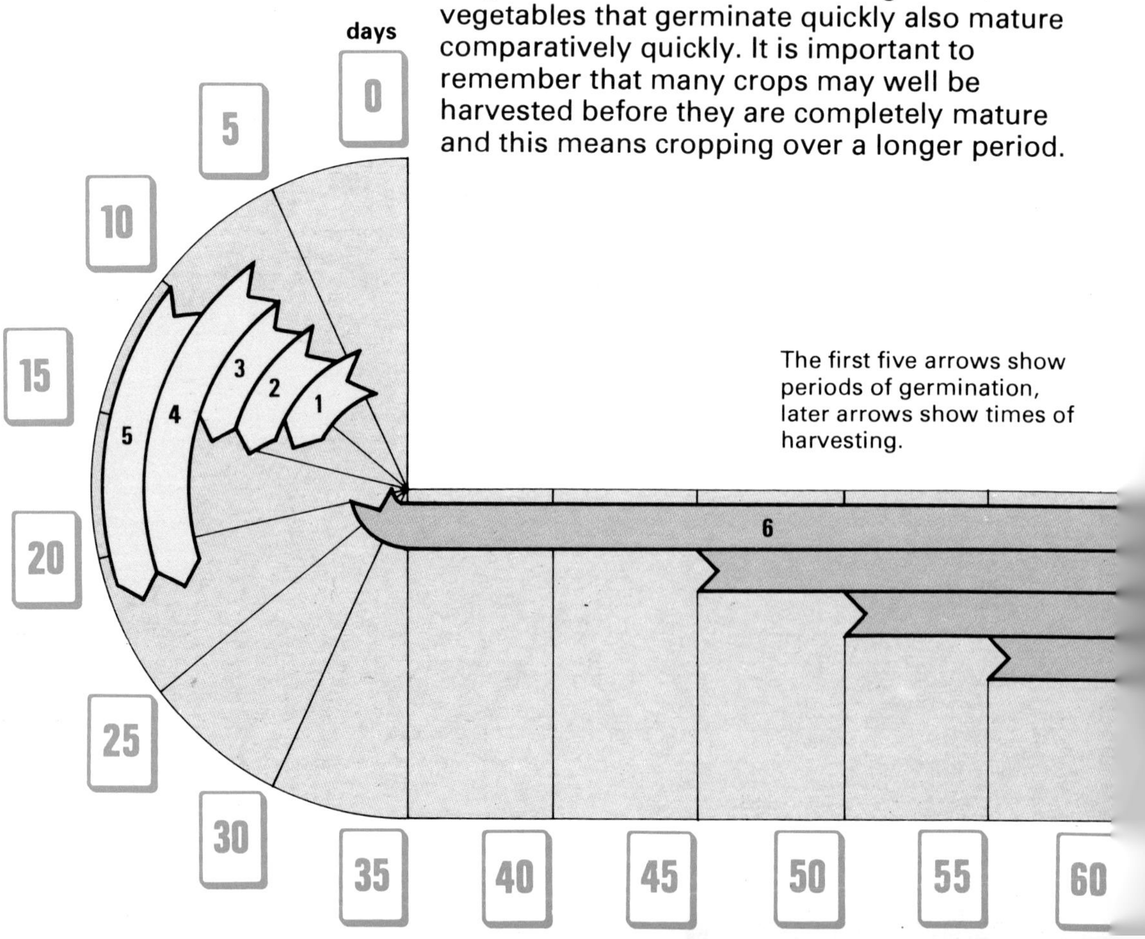

days

0

5

10

15

20

25

30

35

40

45

50

55

60

3

2

1

4

5

6

The first five arrows show periods of germination, later arrows show times of harvesting.

Pelleted seeds take slightly longer to germinate because the protective coating has to be broken down in the soil. It is important to keep the soil moist to help this process.

With the exception of tomatoes and potatoes the really long-maturing vegetables are those which are grown for winter consumption or grow through winter to be harvested in spring.

Harvest root crops carefully if they are to be stored. Hold tops while lifting with a fork or spade. If possible, lift while soil is dry. Fill in and level soil.

The time between when a seed is planted and when it begins to grow varies a lot, depending not only on the kind of seed, but also on the weather. The time during which a crop can be gathered also depends partly on the weather.

1 Lettuce, radishes, marrows (4–12 days)
2 French beans, runner beans, peas, spinach (6–14 days)
3 Beetroot, broccoli, brussels sprouts, cabbage, cauliflower, kale, leeks, onions, shallots, tomatoes (7–14 days)
4 Potatoes (7–21 days)
5 Carrots (10–21 days)
6 Radishes (20–60 days)

7 Lettuce, spinach (45–80 days)
8 Beetroot, marrows (50–75 days)
9 Tomatoes (55–120 days)
10 French beans, runner beans, carrots, kohlrabi, peas, shallots, broccoli, cabbage, cauliflower (60–150 days)
11 Potatoes (90–120 days)
12 Brussels sprouts (100–160 days)

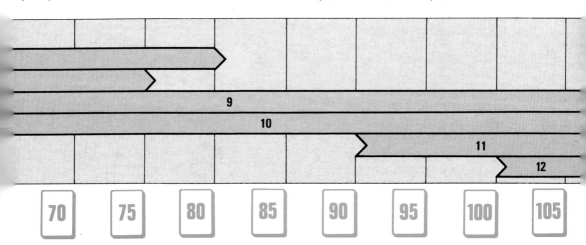

What to hope for

The average yield in pounds and kilograms that can be expected from your seed. Where not otherwise stated the quantity and yield are for a 30 ft (9 m) row.

When planning the crops you will grow in your allotment give careful thought to your family's real needs. You don't want to be embarrassed by having enough lettuces for a regiment, if there are only three or four mouths to feed. It is a waste of space, energy and lettuces. A good general rule is to sow thinly and at intervals to ensure crops of the right size at the right time. Then you will want to take into account the experience of your fellow allotment holders. It may be that the particular lie or quality of the land makes some crops more difficult to grow than others. To avoid overcropping it is important to have some idea of the yield you should expect from your seed. If you are new to the game it may come as a surprise to you that from one tiny seed you can expect to pick 2 lb (0.9 kg) of brussels sprouts or from ¼ oz (7 g) of seed over 30 lb (13.6 kg) of radishes. The chart

Sown	Crop	Yield
4 oz (113 g)	Broad beans	16 lb (7.2 kg)
2 oz (57 g)	French beans	20–30 lb (9–13.5 kg)
4 oz (113 g)	Runner beans	100 lb (45 kg)
¼ oz (7 g)	Beetroot	25 lb (11.3 kg)
1 seed	Broccoli	1½ lb (0.7 kg)
1 seed	Brussels sprouts	2 lb (0.9 kg)
1 seed	Cabbage	1–2½ lb (0.45–1.1 kg)
¼ oz (7 g)	Carrots	25 lb (11.3 kg)
1 seed	Cauliflower	1–2 lb (0.45–0.9 kg)
1 seed	Outdoor cucumber	20 cucumbers
1 seed	Kale	1½ lb (0.7 kg)
⅒ oz (3 g)	Leeks	30 lb (13.6 kg)
⅛ oz (3.5 g)	Lettuce	30 lettuces
60 sets	Onions	24 lb (10.9 kg)
¼ oz (7 g)	Parsnips	30 lb (13.6 kg)
7 oz (198 g)	Peas	30 lb (13.6 kg)
¼ oz (7 g)	Radishes	30 lb (13.6 kg)
½ oz (14 g)	Spinach	20 lb (9 kg)
1 plant	Greenhouse tomatoes	7 lb (3.2 kg)
1 plant	Outdoor tomatoes	4 lb (1.8 kg)
¼ oz (7 g)	Turnips	30 lb (13.6 kg)

illustrates the average yield to be expected with most of the common vegetables – always provided that you follow the rules. Don't forget that some of the vegetables are harvested during the winter months or will keep in store in one form or another.

It was said of a rich mustard manufacturer that he made his fortune not from the mustard people ate but from what they left on their plates. The same could be said about seeds. Often the gardener, having finished his sowing, is left with part-filled packets, and usually he throws them away. He shouldn't, because most seeds have a life expectancy of two years or more, and some last for four, even six, years, as the chart shows. Of course, you can grow from your own seeds: bean, pea and marrow seeds are fairly easy to keep for sowing the next spring.

Let us spray
A gentle syringe with water on your runner bean blossoms will help them to set.

With care, some seeds can be kept for a number of years.

How many years seeds will last

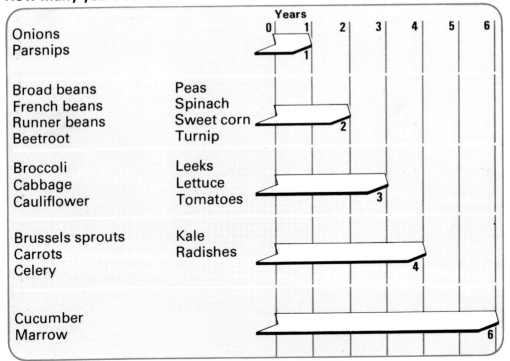

Chapter three
Vegetables

Sixteenth century
gardeners preparing for
spring sowing. Because of
the compact form of their
towns they cultivated strips
of land outside the city
walls.

In this chapter we get down to the growing of
the individual vegetables: the best soil, how to
sow them and when, how to look after them as
they grow, and how long they take to mature.

Some will be seen to be easy, others are more
complicated. Some require a lot of attention,
others can almost be left to look after
themselves.

The major part of this chapter is devoted to
what might be called the 'common or garden'
vegetables – those that you would expect to
find in any allotment. It may be that because of
peculiarities of soil or situation you cannot grow
them all; but you will be able to grow most.

For easy reference we have divided these common or garden vegetables into brassicas, leaf vegetables, root and tuber vegetables, seed vegetables, bulb and stalk vegetables, and vegetable fruits.

The chapter also covers briefly the less common and more exotic vegetables, such as asparagus and aubergine, for which you may be able to find a corner, especially if you are a gourmet.

From all this information you will be able to decide first what you want to grow, and then (by following the simple guide-lines laid down) how to do it, and how to harvest the fruits of your labours. Moreover you will be able to learn something about your vegetables' natural enemies.

Finally there is a section on the more familiar herbs, and don't forget that for these you are not obliged to have a separate herb garden.

Brassicas

CABBAGE (*Brassica*). This popular vegetable is the best-known in the family of brassicas. There are three main kinds of cabbage: the garden or white cabbage, the Savoy, and the red cabbage (the last so called because of its dark purple leaves). Red cabbage is generally used for pickling; the others are used cooked or raw as vegetables. The garden or white cabbage, the most popular, has pale green, heavily veined leaves; the leaves of the Savoy cabbage are wrinkled and a darker green. Cabbages are grown throughout the temperate zones; the plant reaches a height of about 18 in (45 cm) and produces a closely packed head sometimes as large as a football.

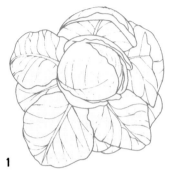

1

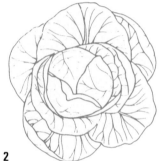

2

1 Autumn and winter varieties (white cabbage)
2 Summer cabbage
3 Spring cabbage
4 Red cabbage

Cabbage
Wheeler's Imperial (early), Durham Early, Greyhound (summer), Drumhead (winter), January King Winter, Ruby Ball (red).
Best soil
Firm soil that has not been recently dug.
Varieties
See above. Some varieties are round-headed, some conical. Savoy cabbages have wrinkled leaves.
Timetable
Germination 7 to 12 days. Summer and winter varieties take 5 to 9 months to mature: spring varieties 9 months.
How to sow
Summer varieties outdoors in April, transplanting in May or June. Winter varieties in May, transplanting in June. Spring varieties in July or August, transplanting in September or October. All in ½ in (1 cm) drills with a firmed-down soil. For transplanting see next page.
Cultivation
Hoe regularly between plants. Keep soil moist. Make sure soil is firmed down in autumn and winter. Liquid feed as plants near harvesting time.
Pests and diseases
See next page for pests. The Club root disease swells roots and eventually destroys the plant. Affected plants should be removed and burned.

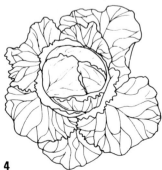

4

The seedlings should be planted out in damp soil when they have 5 or 6 leaves. Use a dibber and water in, firming the soil well. The plants should be about 1½–2 ft (45–60 cm) apart, except spring cabbages, which need only be 6 in (15 cm) apart. Mature spring cabbages require as much space as others but closer planting provides for thinning out as spring greens.

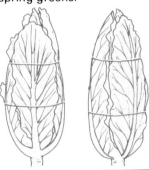

CHINESE CABBAGE (*Brassica chinensis*). Despite their name these vegetables grow rather more like spinach or cos lettuce than like cabbage, but they *did* originate in Asia. The outer leaves can be boiled like cabbage, but the inner, which are crisp and sweet, are eaten raw and are useful in salads. Sow in May or June, possibly as a catch crop, 8 in (20 cm) apart in shallow drills 1 ft (30 cm) apart. Water well. As the heads begin to swell, tie the leaves around as with cos lettuce to help them blanch. They should be firm enough to harvest about 2½ months after sowing.

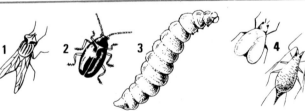

Cabbage pests

1 **Cabbage root fly** Lays small eggs at bottom of stem and roots, turns seedling leaves slightly blue.
2 **Flea beetle** Eats holes in seedling leaves.
3 **Cutworm** Eats into stem at soil level.
4 **White- and greenfly** Attack leaves.
5 **Caterpillar of cabbage butterfly** Devours leaves.
6 **Cabbage gall weevil** Deposits eggs in roots, which swell.

Treatment

1 To prevent, dust soil around seedling with calomel dust when 1 in (2 cm) high, and again after transplanting.
2 As with **1**, but using derris dust.
3 Rake in Bromophos on soil surface.
4 Spray liquid derris or apply derris dust.
5 Crush eggs, remove caterpillars, and apply derris dust.
6 To prevent, treat as for root fly, **1**.

Brassicas

BRUSSELS SPROUTS (*Brassica oleracea bullata gemmifera*). A member of the cabbage family, this plant grows to a height of about 3 ft (1 m). Small buds like miniature cabbages form up the stalk, and these are harvested as a winter vegetable. As the lower sprouts are picked others develop higher up the stalk, providing a continuing crop.

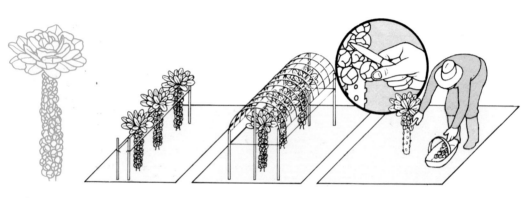

Earthing up and firming the soil in the autumn generally provides sufficient support, but where exposed, taller varieties should be staked.

Protect from slugs and birds. Always pick sprouts from the bottom upwards, a few from each plant. When the sprouts are exhausted, the top makes a cabbage substitute.

Brussels Sprouts
Peer Gynt, Fillbasket, Early Dwarf, Market Rearguard (late).
Best soil
Firm and containing plenty of organic matter.
Varieties
Ordinary varieties produce largest sprouts and growth is drawn out . F1 hybrid varieties produce tighter-packed sprouts over a shorter period.
Timetable
Sow early varieties for autumn and winter crops (October, November, December) in second half of March, planting out in May. Sow later varieties in April, planting out in June for late winter crop (January, February, March).
How to sow
Thinly in a shallow ½ in (1 cm) drill. Transplant when seedlings are about 6 in (15 cm) high about 2 ft (60 cm) apart in rows 2½ ft (75 cm) apart. Water in with lowest leaves at soil level and firm soil well.
Cultivation
Regular hoeing between plants, watering in dry weather. Earth up and firm soil in autumn.
Pests and diseases
At first sign of caterpillars crush egg patches and spray with solution of handful of salt in a pail of water or dust with derris powder. Clubroot, remove plant and burn. Aphids (greenfly and blackfly), spray with derris.

BROCCOLI (*Brassica oleracea*). This plant is similar to the cauliflower but the flower clusters that form the head are less closely packed. It grows to a height of about 2 ft (60 cm). The shoots or spears that carry the flower clusters are cut before the flowers have opened to provide a succulent vegetable. The green-sprouting variety is called Calabrese or Italian broccoli.

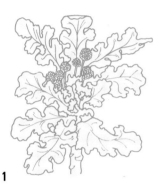

1 White and purple sprouting broccoli
2 Calabrese or Italian broccoli

2

Never allow the flower buds on broccoli spears to open. If they do, further spears will not be produced.
Always be sure that the soil is thoroughly moist before mulching between plants. Don't use fresh grass-cuttings.

Broccoli
Green Comet (head), Italian Sprouting (green spears), Purple Sprouting (Christmas, Early and Late), White Sprouting (Early and Late).
Best soil
Firm and containing plenty of organic matter.
Varieties
Purple-sprouting, white-sprouting, and green-sprouting (Calabrese or Italian). Calabrese are ready first (August to October), then purple (December to April), then white (March to May).
Timetable
Germination from 7 to 12 days. Harvesting 4 months for Calabrese, 9 to 10 months for purple and white varieties.
How to sow
Thinly in the open in ½ in (1 cm) drills in March and April. Firm down soil. Transplant 2 ft (60 cm) apart when about 3 in (7 cm) high, watering in.
Cultivation
Regular hoeing between plants, watering in dry weather and mulching between plants. Draw up soil in autumn and firm down, staking if site is exposed to wind. Occasional application of fertiliser. To harvest, cut flower shoots when firmly formed, beginning with centre shoot.
Pests and diseases
See Brussels sprouts.

Brassicas

CAULIFLOWER (*Brassica oleracea botrytis cauliflora*). Unlike the cabbage (which nevertheless is a close relative), the cauliflower, instead of forming a tightly packed head of leaves, produces a packed head of close white flowers on short stems. This head is enclosed in short and then larger green leaves, most of which are usually stripped from the head before cooking.

To prevent the plant from being rocked by autumn winds, carefully bank up soil around the base.
To protect from frost, remove some soil from north side of plant and (without uplifting roots) heel it over so that curd faces north. Cover stem with removed soil.

Cauliflower
Early Snowball (summer), Polaris (late summer), White Heart (autumn), All-the-Year-Round.
Best soil
Previously manured, well dug and well settled.
Varieties
Summer, sown outdoors early April, transplant in June or July; autumn, sown April or May, transplant in June or July; winter, sown May, transplant in July.
Timetable
Germination 7 to 12 days: summer varieties mature in 4½ to 6 months, winter varieties in 10 months. Do not wait until all curds are fully grown: cut some while small or you will have an embarrassment of riches.
How to sow
Outdoors in shallow ½ in (1 cm) drills when soil is moist. Transplant when seedlings have 5 or 6 leaves, about 2 ft (60 cm) apart.
Cultivation
Regular hoeing to keep down weeds. Keep well watered and feed occasionally. When curd develops in summer, bend outer leaves over to protect it from the sun.
Pests and diseases
As with other brassicas – cabbage root fly, club root, cabbage caterpillar etc.

KALE (*Brassica oleracea var. acephala*)

Sometimes also called colewort, this tough member of the cabbage family has thick leaves with a curly fringe; these do not form a compact head as does the cabbage, but are on separate stems. Only tender young leaves and shoots should be used in cooking, because the larger leaves are bitter to the taste.

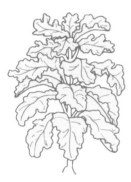

Kale is easy to grow and hardy. Like all brassicas it likes well-firmed soil, plenty of water and freedom from weeds.

Kale
Pentland Brig, Dwarf Green-curled, Verdure.

Best soil
Well-drained and firm. Kale does not demand a rich soil.

Varieties
Most popular are the curly-leaved and leaf-and-spear varieties and rape kale, which is exceptionally hardy.

Timetable
Germination 7 to 12 days. Sow early varieties in April, later varieties in May. The former mature in about 7½ months and the latter in 9 months.

How to sow
Outdoors in April and May in ½ in (1 cm) drills. Transplant in moist soil when seedlings are about 6 in (15 cm) tall, leaving plants 2 ft (60 cm) apart. Firm down surrounding soil well. Rape kale varieties should be sown where they are to remain and thinned out when ready.

Cultivation
Keep earth well firmed but well hoed. Earth up stems in autumn. Keep well watered. When transplanting apply a little derris dust to surrounding soil.

Pests and diseases
Kale is liable to the pests and diseases of the brassica family but is so tough and hardy that it is more resistant than the other members.

Leaf vegetables

LETTUCE (*Lactuca sativa*). There are several varieties of this popular vegetable, which provides the basis of most salads. Best-known are the cabbage lettuce (*Lactuca crispa*) – which can be about the same size as a cabbage but whose leaves are not so tightly packed and are lighter and more delicate – and the cos or romaine lettuce (*Lactuca longiflora*) – which has darker, crisper leaves growing in a sheaf. There are two varieties of cabbage lettuce: those with soft and smooth leaves, (either quick or long growing), and those with crisp, curled leaves.

Growing techniques

Lettuces are easy to grow and not demanding on the gardener but points to remember are:

1 Sow periodically in small amounts – say, every fortnight – to ensure a succession. By sowing smooth-leaved and crisp varieties at the same time you should achieve a succession, because their maturing periods differ.

2 It is best to sow where they are to grow and thin out to 9–12 in (22–30 cm).

3 But lettuce can be transplanted, when the first real leaves have formed. Remember transplanting checks growth.

Lettuce
Cabbage: Webb's Wonder, Valdor, Buttercrunch. *Cos*: Winter Density, Lobjoit's Green, Little Gem.

Best soil
Fine, moist and non-acid, preferably composted in previous autumn.

Varieties
Cos, cabbage (smooth and crisp), and open-leaved. Cabbage variety mature quicker.

Timetable
Germination 7 to 12 days. Sow outdoors from late March to late July to crop from June to October.

How to sow
In open in ½ in (1 cm) drills 1 ft (30 cm) apart, firming down soil. For early seedlings, in frame or greenhouse. Sow small quantities at regular intervals.

Cultivation
Protect young plants from slugs and birds; hoe to keep weed-free. Watch for signs of hearts 'bolting,' i.e. growing upwards. Use at once or throw on compost.

Pests and diseases
Slugs and birds. Mosaic disease, spread by greenfly, shows in stunted growth and mottled leaves. Grey mould rots stem at soil level but is most frequently found in plants grown under glass.

4 Lettuce matures rather quickly so to save space it can be intercropped – grown between slower-maturing vegetables such as peas.

5 Early seedlings can be brought on in seed trays in frames or greenhouses. Later seeds sown in the open can be advanced by putting under cloches when planting out.

6 Slugs love the tender young seedlings so protect them with slug pellets. Also protect from birds.

7 Spray early against greenfly, which can spread mosaic disease.

If heads of cos and cabbage lettuce feel firm when pressed lightly at the top they are ready for picking. Pull up the whole plant when crisp in the early morning or evening and remove roots and outer leaves.

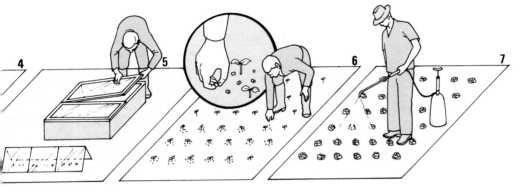

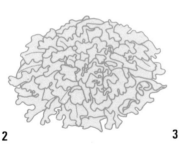

1

2

3

Varieties: Cabbage lettuce is round-headed, either soft and smooth-leaved (**1**) or with crisp curled leaves (**2**); Cos lettuce (**3**) is tall, dark-leaved and pointed; and loose-leaved lettuce does not form a heart (**4**).

4

Leaf vegetables

1 Spinach
2 Spinach beet

SPINACH (*Spinacia oleracea*). This vegetable has large, thick, dark green, succulent leaves and is a prolific cropper, particularly rich in vitamins. The plant grows to between 1½ and 2 ft (45–60 cm) high. The popular spinach beet (*Beta vulgaris var. cicla*), also called perpetual spinach, is not a true member of the spinach family and is related to the sugar beet, but its leaves are used in much the same way as real spinach.

Spinach
Longstanding Round, King of Denmark, New Zealand Prickly.
Best soil
Well dug, rich and well composted. Perpetual spinach is not so demanding.
Varieties
Perpetual spinach yields from July for about 9 months; summer; winter.
Timetable
Sow perpetual spinach in April to harvest in summer, autumn and winter; summer spinach from March to July to harvest June to September; and winter spinach in August and September for winter picking. Germination 2 to 3 weeks.
How to sow
In ½ in (1 cm) drills, 1 ft (30 cm) apart or between higher-growing vegetables. Thin to about 6 in (15 cm) apart.
Cultivation
Regular hoeing. Ensure soil is moist. Spray if affected by greenfly. Cut and use outer leaves while young to ensure continuing growth. Protect winter spinach from frost.

CELTUCE (*Lactuca sativa var. angustana*) is a variety of lettuce, but grows on a stalk. It must be well watered to keep the leaves tender.

CORN SALAD (*Valerianella locusta*) is a very hardy plant, but requires a rich soil.

SORREL (*Rumex acetosa*) has a sharp taste, because it contains some oxalic acid. It is usually eaten in salads.

SWISS CHARD (*beta cicla*). As its Latin name shows, this is a member of the beetroot family; but it looks something like rhubarb, with either white or crimson stems and rich, dark green, sometimes red-tinted, leaves. The leaves are cooked like spinach and the white stems can be used like asparagus.

Swiss chard is sown like beetroot in the open in April in 1 in (2 cm) drills 18 in (45 cm) apart, and thinned out later to 1 ft (30 cm) apart. A second sowing may be made in July. As with rhubarb, pull – don't cut – the sticks.

GOOD KING HENRY (*Chenopodium bonus-Henricus*). As its name indicates this vegetable has a long history. It could be known as 'poor man's asparagus', for its young shoots are not unlike the aristocrat of vegetables. It is a perennial, grows to a height of about 2 ft (60 cm) and has long-stemmed arrow-shaped leaves. Sow seeds in April in shallow drills and transplant to 12 in (30 cm) apart. When the shoots appear, earth them up to blanch the base and cut them when they are still young – about 5–6 in (12–15 cm) high. They are cooked like asparagus and served with butter or mayonnaise. In the autumn, mulch the plants to bring new growth the following spring.

ENDIVE (*Cichorium endivia*). Although it is related to chicory, endive is grown like lettuces and eaten raw in salads in the same way. Its flavour is slightly more bitter. There are two varieties – curly endive and escarole. The former has curled, jagged leaves and is blanched by covering the crown of the head against the sun. Escarole has broader and smoother leaves.

This vegetable likes a heavy, moist soil. Sow at intervals in shallow ½ in (1 cm) drills, thinning to about 8 in (20 cm) apart. Keep well fed and well watered. Escarole is blanched by tying the leaves firmly together.

MUSTARD (*Sinapis alba*) and CRESS (*Lepidium sativum*). These two vegetables combined are used in salads and for garnish and can be grown easily and quickly all the year round. They may be grown in winter in boxes on the windowsill or in the allotment or garden in small beds. Beds should have a fine tilth and the seed is sown broadcast, not in rows. The mustard seed should be sown 4 days after the cress because it matures more quickly. Both should be ready to cut in 2 weeks or so.

Root and tuber vegetables

CARROT (*Daucus carota*). This highly nutritious vegetable is grown for its pinkish-orange roots, which may be short, intermediate or long. They may be eaten cooked or raw and store well. The foliage is fern-like. Carrots are fairly easy to cultivate but require particular attention when being thinned out to restrict the attentions of the carrot fly. A good tip is to sow them next to onions. The carrot fly dislikes the smell of onions, and the onion fly that of carrots.

Short-rooted (either cylindrical or round); intermediate-rooted (most popular maincrop); long-rooted.

Mutual dislike
Sow the onions next to the carrots. The smell of each deters the fly of the other.

Carrot
Early Nantes (short-rooted), Short'n'Sweet, Autumn King (medium), Favourite (Medium).
Best soil
Light, deep loam not recently manured.
Varieties
See above. Short-rooted provide early crops, intermediate maincrop and for storage, long-rooted also maincrop.
Timetable
Germination period 2 weeks. Maincrop matures in about 4 months, early in 3½ months. Early varieties should be sown from March onwards, later varieties from April to July.
How to sow
In the open from March in shallow ½ in (1 cm) drills, 9 in (22 cm) apart for earlies, 1 ft (30 cm) apart for maincrop. Thin eventually to about 3 in (7 cm) apart. Some thinnings can be used in the kitchen. Firm down soil after thinning to discourage carrot fly.
Cultivation
Keep well hoed against weeds, watering in dry weather.
Pests and diseases
Greenfly and carrot fly. The former attack the leaves, the latter (symptom reddish leaves) the root.

Sowing

Early carrots can be brought on in a hot frame or bed, sowing in January in loam with peat and coarse sand. When sowing outdoors dust drills with insecticide to discourage carrot fly.

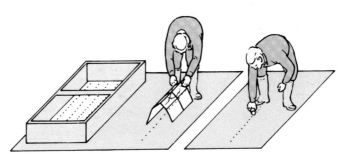

Care and pests

Dust or spray with derris if attacked by greenfly (a). After thinning out, be sure to firm down soil to prevent carrot fly penetrating through broken earth, and to remove thinnings (b), which attract carrot fly if left lying around.

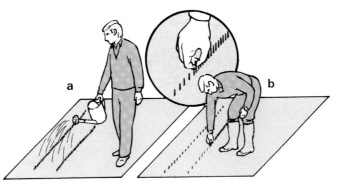

Harvesting

Small carrots can be pulled by hand (a). Use a fork to lift larger ones (b). If storing, remove foliage to about ½ in (1 cm) above crown of root and remove any soil.

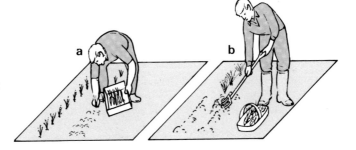

Storing

Indoors between layers of sand and peat in a wooden box. Outdoors packed in a pointed heap covered with straw and a 4 in (10 cm layer of soil (called a clamp). a Wisp of straw should be left obtruding from the top to ventilate.

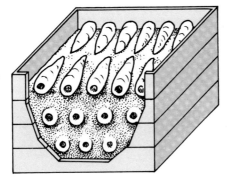

Root and tuber vegetables

BEETROOT (*Beta vulgaris var. crassa*). Although beetroot is grown for its edible root, its young leaves, cooked like spinach, can be used as a vegetable. The plant, distinguished by its red-veined leaves, grows to a height of about 15 in (37 cm) and may have a globular, conical or cylindrical root, usually red, sometimes white or golden. There are two forms of seed, cluster and monogerm. Clusters consist of several seeds, monogerm has only one.

Sow seeds in small clusters along the row. Carefully hoe while seedlings are young. When harvesting chop off the tops not too near the crown.

Beetroot
Crimson Globe, Detroit Globe, Boltardy (globe), Cylindra (cylindrical), Long Blood Red (long).
Best soil
On the sandy side, well-worked but not recently manured.
Varieties
Globe (most popular); long; tankard or cylindrical (grown for winter storage).
Timetable
For early crop sow in March under glass; outdoors in second half of April for harvesting from July. Germination 2 to 3 weeks. Maturing time 2¼ months -4 months.
How to sow
Custer seed variety: 3 in (7 cm) apart in drills about 1 in (2 cm) deep and 1 ft (30 cm) apart. When clusters of seedlings appear thin out to one in each, eventually thinning to 6 in (15 cm) apart. Single seed variety: thinly in drills about 1 in (2 cm) deep and 1 ft (30 cm) apart. Thin out to 3 in (7 cm) apart, finally to 6 in (15 cm).
Cultivation
Straightforward. Keep weed-free (avoiding touching roots with hoe) and well-watered in dry weather.
Pests and diseases
Usually fairly free. Mangold fly or flea beetle may attack the leaves. Nicotine dust for the former, derris for the latter.

PARSNIP (*Pastinacea sativa*). Easily grown both commercially and in allotments and gardens, this plant has a long, tapering, yellowish-white edible root. It is cooked as a vegetable and in stews and soups, and can be left in the ground in winter. It is a biennial plant and easy to grow; but if neglected it can become a troublesome weed.

If you are not using pelleted seeds choose a still day to sow your parsnips; the seeds are very light and easily blow away. Lime the soil to protect against parsnip canker.

In stony ground, help the young roots by first making a hole before sowing. Alternatively sow in upright pipes filled with sieved soil and peat.

Parsnip
Avonresister (short), Offenham (medium), Tender and True (long).

Best soil
Deep for long varieties. Not recently manured, because manure causes the roots to fork, as also may stony or lumpy soil.

Varieties
Short-rooted (does not require such good soil); intermediate-rooted; long-rooted (requires very deep soil).

Timetable
Sow in late February or March. Short-rooted variety can be sown as late as April. Germination 3 to 4 weeks; maturing time 8 months.

How to sow
In open in ½ in (1 cm) drills 1 ft (30 cm) apart. Sow seeds in small clusters about 8 in (20 cm) apart, thinning to one plant when large enough to handle.

Cultivation
Straightforward. Keep weed-free. Roots can be lifted when foliage collapses in autumn, but parsnips can be left in the ground all winter.

Pests and diseases
Parsnip canker causes shoulders of roots to crack, and go brown and then rotten. Destroy affected plants.

Root and tuber vegetables

TURNIP (*Brassica rapa var. rapifera*). A welcome ingredient in stews and soups, this vegetable is grown mainly for its usually globular root. This has a thick greenish-white skin and rather coarse white flesh with a strong flavour when cooked. Although it is grown for the root, its leaves, when young and tender, are used as winter greens.

Turnips need to be grown quickly to enhance their flavour so the soil for early varieties should be well composted or manured and well firmed down.

1 Turnip
2 Swede

Turnip
Tokyo Cross (early), Snowball (early), Golden Ball (main)
Best soil
Fine and moist, manured for a previous crop.
Varieties
Early (flat, cylindrical and globe); maincrop (globe).
Maincrop varieties can be stored through the winter.
Timetable
Germination 7 to 10 days; maturing time 2 to 3 months.
Earlies sown in April should be ready in July. Maincrop sown in July ready from October onwards.
How to sow
Outdoors in ½ in (1 cm) drills at intervals of 3 weeks from April to July. Thin out when large enough to handle to 6 in (15 cm) apart (early) or 10 in (25 cm) (maincrop). Drills should be 15 in (37 cm) apart.
Cultivation
Keep well hoed and watered in dry conditions. Lift early turnips while still fairly small.
Pests and diseases
Fairly free. Turnip flea beetle attacks young turnips, eating the leaves: dust with derris powder.

RADISH (*Raphanus sativus*). A member of the mustard family, with its characteristic hot flavour, the summer radish is one of the smallest of the root vegetables. It grows quickly and is a popular vegetable in most allotments and gardens for its use as a relish in salads. It is a cruciferous plant, i.e. its blossom has four equal petals in the form of a cross. The small round or tube-shaped root is generally red or white in colour.

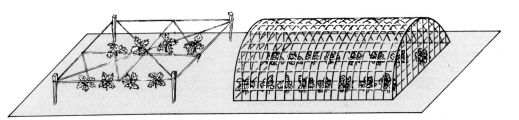

Protect against birds. Simple string can be as effective as expensive caging.

Radish
French Breakfast, Scarlet Globe.
Best soil
Well composted with a fine tilth. Top dress with general fertiliser.
Varieties
Summer varieties, round, intermediate and long-rooted; winter variety much larger and less frequently grown.
Timetable
Germination 4 to 7 days. Maturing time 3 weeks to 1½ months (summer), 2½ months (winter). Can be sown under cloches in February, outdoors from March onwards.
How to sow
Winter varieties are sown in high summer.
Outdoors in shallow ½ in (1 cm) drills, 6 in (15 cm) apart, firming down soil well. Sow thinly regularly, thinning out to about 1 in (2 cm) apart. Winter varieties should be spaced 6 in (15 cm) apart.
Cultivation
Hoe regularly, weed by hand and water if dry. Summer radishes germinate and mature very quickly and can be grown as a catch crop — i.e. grown where later vegetables are to grow.
Pests and diseases
Flea beetles eat leaves: dust drills with derris dust.

Root and tuber vegetables

POTATO (*Solanum tuberosum*). This is one of the world's most important vegetables. The plant, belonging to the nightshade family, has dark green leaves and white, purple or yellow flowers and grows to an average height of 2–3 ft (60–90 cm). The potato tubers grow at the end of stems that develop from the underground part of the stem. Potatoes are good as an initial crop in any allotment as the soil benefits from being turned over.

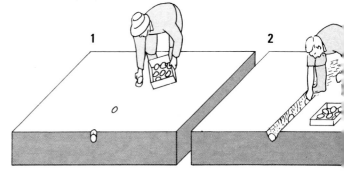

Varieties
Early potatoes are smaller, more easily peeled and have a finer flavour than maincrop, which can be stored.

Potato
Early: Arran Pilot, Duke of York. *Maincrop*: King Edward, Majestic, Pentland Crown, Desirée.
Best soil
Potatoes grow in almost any soil and like the sun.
Varieties
Early varieties for 'new' potatoes in the spring and summer; maincrop for autumn and winter.
Timetable
Plant early potatoes in late March if mild, to harvest in June. Maincrop in April to harvest in September or Ocotober. When haulms die down maincrop can be harvested and stored.
How to sow
They are grown from seed potatoes, which are planted out where they are to grow, by any of the methods shown.
Cultivation
Once foliage shows, begin to earth up with a draw hoe, because uncovered potatoes go green and are uneatable. Continue earthing up as the plants grow so that you have a fairly wide ridge in dry weather.
Pests and diseases
Wireworm can bore holes in tubers. Potato blight causes tubers to rot in store.

Bordeaux mixture, home made
Bordeaux mixture is used as a precaution against potato blight. You can make it yourself by dissolving 3 oz (84 g) of copper sulphate in 1 gall (4.6 l) of hot water in a plastic bucket. Leave overnight. Stir 4 oz (113 g) of slaked lime into 1 gall (4.6 l) of cold water, mix the two and spray on the haulms.

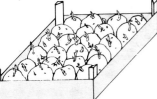

Seeding
Seed potatoes should be prepared for planting by 'chitting', i.e. packing them in shallow boxes – egg boxes will do – and keeping them in light, cool surroundings to help the shoots grow sturdily. The potatoes should be packed with the 'rose-end' – the end with most eyes – upwards.

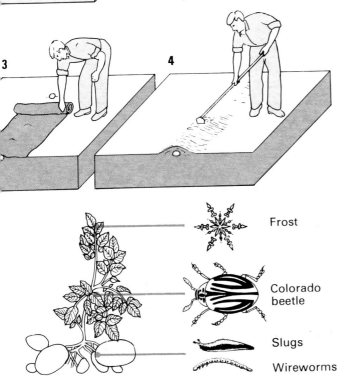

Frost

Colorado beetle

Slugs

Wireworms

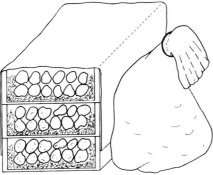

There are different ways of planting potatoes:
1   With a trowel make 5 in (12 cm) deep holes, 1 ft (30 cm) apart for earlies, 15 in (37 cm) for maincrop. Place seed potato, sprout end upwards, in hole, fill with soil. Rows should be 2 ft (60 cm) (earlies) or 2½ ft (75 cm) (maincrop) apart.
2   Dig trench about 5 in (12 cm) deep, and place seed potatoes in it spaced as for 1 above. Return earth to trench.
3   Use black polythene sheets about 2 ft (60 cm) wide. Press seed potatoes into soil about ½ in (1 cm), sprout end upwards. Lay polythene over, making cuts in it to allow foliage to push through.
4   Sow as for 3, drawing up soil to form a ridge.

Enemies
Frost affects young foliage: protect it by earthing up. Slugs and wireworm can damage tubers by tunnelling into them. Potato blight causes brown patches on leaves and eventually rots tubers. Potato wart disease shows with wart-like growth on tubers: destroy affected plants. Colorado beetle attack the leaves of the plant: report all cases.

Storing
Potatoes can be stored outdoors in clamps (i.e. covered with straw and then earth) or indoors in straw-lined boxes. Be sure to cover with paper or sacking, because if light gets to them tubers will go green. Or they can be stored in sacks: if plastic bags are used make a few small breathing holes.

Root and tuber vegetables

This page shows several varieties of root and tuber vegetables which are less popular with gardeners in the UK. Many of these varieties are grown and enjoyed more widely in Europe, and they can provide a welcome change from the usual types of root and tuber vegetables. Like all root crops, they need lots of rich soil.

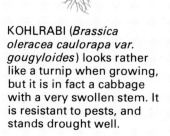

CELERIAC (*Apium graveolens var. rapaceum*). This form of celery is sometimes called turnip-rooted celery, which describes it well. The stems and foliage look like celery but the base is swollen and may weigh several pounds. It has a similar flavour to celery. Unlike celery, it does not need to be trenched or earthed up. Sow in boxes in a hot frame or green house, planting out seedlings in the open 12 in (30 cm) apart in rows 18 in (45 cm) apart. The swollen base should rest on the soil, which should be well manured and in a sunny position. Water well and feed well with liquid manure from July onwards. Remove any lateral shoots. Lift the roots as needed from October.

KOHLRABI (*Brassica oleracea caulorapa var. gougyloides*) looks rather like a turnip when growing, but it is in fact a cabbage with a very swollen stem. It is resistant to pests, and stands drought well.

ARTICHOKE (JERUSALEM) (*Helianthus tuberosus*). Quite unlike the globe artichoke, this plant is a member of the sunflower family and grows to 10 ft (3 m) or more in height but rarely blooms. It has potato-like roots with a knobbly surface, which can be cooked and eaten like potatoes and are often made into soup. It is grown from tubers planted about 6 in (15 cm) deep, 12 in (30 cm) apart, in February and March in fertile, well-manured soil. The tubers are lifted when the tops die down in the autumn, and can be stored. Replant tubers to provide further crops.

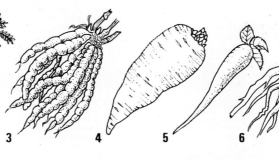

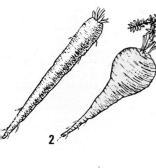

Above are six root vegetables that are well known in various parts of Europe, but infrequently grown in the UK.

1 Scorzonera (*Scorzonera hispanica*)
2 Hamburg parsley (*Petroselinum crispum*)
3 Skirret (*Sium sisarum*)
4 Chervil (*Chaerophyllum bulbosum*)
5 Rampion (*Campanula rapunculus*)
6 Scolymus (*Scolymus hispanica*)

SALSIFY (*Tragopogon porrifolius*). This vegetable, with its brown, carrot-like, tapering roots, is sometimes called the Oyster Plant because its flavour when cooked is reminiscent of that of oysters. It is eaten as a vegetable or used to flavour soups. It is easy to grow, liking the sun and light soil. It should be sown in April in 1 in (2 cm) drills with 2 or 3 seeds at 9 in (22 cm) intervals, thinning out to leave the strongest seedling. It is the roots that are eaten and they can be left in the ground until needed.

CHINESE ARTICHOKES (*Stachys affinis*) are not related to either of the other kinds of artichokes. They are also easy to grow, and (like Jerusalem artichokes) sometimes hard to get rid of.

When hoeing and lifting root vegetables, care should be taken not to cut the roots; this not only spoils their appearance, but is also wasteful.

Seed vegetables

1 French beans
2 Broad beans
3 Runner beans

BEANS. These are members of the family of leguminous plants, which also includes peas and other plants whose seeds are contained in pods. There are several varieties for allotment and garden; all have kidney-shaped seeds or beans. They include the French bean (*Phaseolus vulgaris*), a plant with a long thin pod that grows to a height of 2 ft (60 cm); the broad bean (*Vicia faba*), a taller plant with larger, light-coloured seeds; and the scarlet runner or runner bean (*Phaseolus multiflorus*), which grows to a height of 8 ft (2.5 m) or more and bears vivid scarlet blossoms and long succulent pods.

1

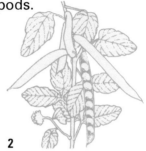

2

3

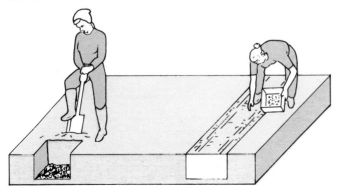

It helps to sow broad beans in 2 in (5 cm) drills about 9 in (22 cm) apart, forming a double row and separated from the next double row by 2 ft (60 cm). This helps staking. French beans are sown also 9 in (22 cm) apart in 2 in (5 cm) drills 2 ft (60 cm) apart. Broad beans can be sown Oct/Nov if the ground is dry, making the crop more resistant to blackfl

For runner beans it is best to dig a trench about 18 in (45 cm) wide and dig in plenty of manure or compost, then refill the trench with soil. Beans are then sown on each side (i.e. about 15 in (37 cm) apart) in 2 in (4 cm) drills. The beans should be about 10 in (25 cm) apart.

Sow what!
*Don't soak runner beans
before sowing.
Don't sow broad beans
with holes in them.
Don't sow French beans
in cold soil.*

1 Broad beans can be supported by planting stakes along the rows and stringing between as shown. **2 French beans** usually grow to only between 1 and 2 ft (30–60 cm) although there are climbers. **3 Runner beans** grow to 8–10 ft (2.5–3 m) and climb naturally up poles, canes or string. (See next page).

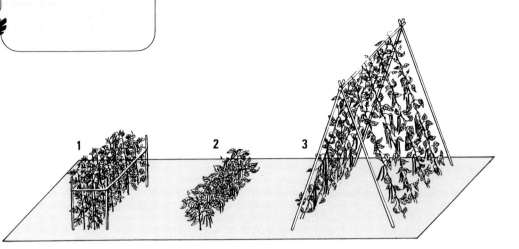

French Beans	The Prince, Masterpiece, Limelight (early).
Broad Beans	Red Epicure, Bunyard's Exhibition (autumn sowing), Masterpiece Major (spring sowing).
Runner Beans	Scarlet Emperor, Crusader, Kelvedon Marvel (early).
Best soil	Beans do not like heavy acid soils. French and Runner beans need well-manured ground.
Varieties	Broad, French and runner beans are most common.
Timetable	Broad beans germinate in 10 to 14 days, and mature in 4 months (unless autumn sown). French beans germinate in 2 to 3 weeks, maturing in 2½ to 3 months. Runners germinate in 10 to 14 days, and mature in 3 to 3½ months.
How to sow	Broad beans 9 in (22 cm) apart in 2 in (5 cm) drills about 1 ft (30 cm) apart (see next page). French beans 9 in (22 cm) apart in 2 in (5 cm) drills 2 ft (60 cm) apart. Runners in 2 in (4 cm) drills on each side of a refilled trench.
Cultivation	Regular hoeing and watering. With broad beans nip 3 in (7 cm) off top of stem when beans start to form. Stake if necessary. French beans (except climbers) don't require support but pieces of twig help. Runner beans must be allowed to climb and can be helped by tying seedlings to canes. 'Stop' runners when they reach the tops of the canes. Spray flowers of French and runner beans with water to help beans to set. Pick beans while small to ensure continuing crops.
Pests and diseases	Protect seedlings from slugs. Protect broad and French beans from blackfly. Guard against mice eating seed rows.

Seed vegetables

Different Ways of
Supporting Runner Beans.

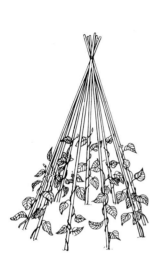

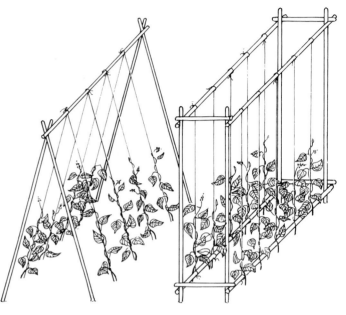

The long poles or canes
supporting runner beans
are susceptible to high
winds and have a heavy
load to carry. Make sure
they are buried at least 1 ft
(30 cm) in the ground and
well firmed in. Use stout
twine to tie them securely.
When plants have reached
the top, pinch out the
growing point.

Beware of mice, which work
along the rows eating the
seed. Watch out for slugs
eating seedlings. Broad
beans are susceptible to
blackfly.

1 Blackfly
2 Slug
3 Mouse

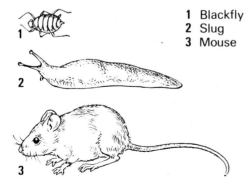

1
2
3

The power of the Press
*Before sowing or
planting runner beans
put a layer of wet
newspaper in the bottom
of the trench. It helps to
keep the soil damp.*

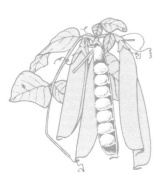

PEA (*Pisum sativum*). This is one of the most delectable of vegetables. No shop-bought or packaged peas can equal the flavour of those freshly picked from an allotment or garden. As its tendrils show, the pea is a climbing plant. Its fruit consists of pods containing peas that swell as the pods ripen. Different varieties can grow from 18 in (45 cm) to 5 ft (1.5 m) high and peas can be harvested from early June to September.

The seedlings should be protected from birds by stretching black threads across; when the seedlings are a few inches high encourage them to climb with small twigs; the traditional way of supporting peas is with peasticks.

Root cause
When crop is harvested throw stem and leaves on compost but leave roots in the ground, because they feed nitrogen back into the soil.

Pea
Early: 1½ to 2 feet Little Marvel, Kelvedon Wonder, Feltham First; 2–3 feet Onward, Pilot. *Late* Senator, Achievement (3–4 ft)

Best soil
Well dug and composted the previous autumn.

Varieties
Round-seeded; wrinkled seeded (sweet); mangetout (the pods can also be eaten).

Timetable
Germination 7 to 10 days: maturing time 3 to 4 months. Sow for succession from March to June.

How to sow
Either in single drills 2 in (5 cm) deep or in double or treble rows at the same depth in a 6 in (15 cm) *wide* drill. Drills should be 2–3 ft (60–90 cm) apart. Sow a handful at the end of the row to make up any gaps.

Cultivation
Keep weed-free and well watered, mulching occasionally. Taller varieties will need to be supported by peasticks or plastic netting. Harvest when pods are young and plump, picking from bottom upwards. Take care not to uproot .

Pests and diseases
Pea moth larvae eat into pods; mice can eat seed rows; pea mildew turns leaves white; thrips distort pods.

Seed vegetables

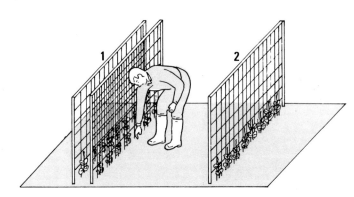

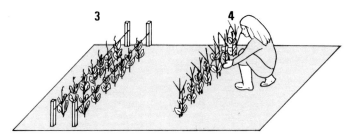

Different ways of supporting peas: **(1)** between two plastic nets; **(2)** with one plastic net; **(3)** by string on either side; **(4)** with peasticks.

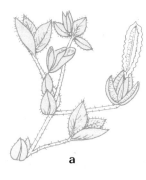

a

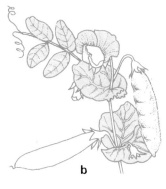

b

c

Something in hand
When sowing beans or peas sow a few extra at the end of the row. The plants are very useful for filling any gaps in the rows.

There are various other varieties of peas that you may like to try growing. The Asparagus pea (*Lotus tetragonolobus*) (a) is not a member of the pea family, and tastes slightly of asparagus. The sugar pea or *mangetout* (*Pisum sativum var. charatum*) (b) is popular because the pods can be eaten too. And the *petit pois* (c) is the finest variety of peas.

SWEET CORN (*Zea mays rugosa*). Sometimes known as corn on the cob, sweet corn is a variety of maize. The cobs, or ears, grow on stems that can grow in height to 6 ft (2 m) or more. The cobs consist of large tightly packed yellow grains enclosed in a sheaf of leaves. The plants fertilise themselves, the male tassel at the top of the plant shedding pollen on the female tufts of silk at the tip of each cob.

Sweet corn is sown in blocks rather than in rows, to assist in pollination by the wind.
Tie up firmly as the plants grow. When harvesting twist out the cob from its position.

Sweetcorn	North Star, Kelvedon Glory.
Best soil	Sheltered site exposed to the sun with well-drained soil, previously manured.
Varieties	Safest to grow are the F1 hybrids, of which there are early and late varieties.
Timetable	Germination time 10 to 12 days. Maturing time about 4 months.
How to sow	Outdoors, only after all risk of frost has gone, in 1 in (2 cm) drills 18 in (45 cm) apart to form a rectangular block. Sow three seeds 1 ft (30 cm) apart along drills removing weakest seedlings to leave strongest one. Can also be sown in pots under glass and planted out when all danger of frost has passed.
Cultivation	Prop roots will appear at the base of the stalk and these should be covered by soil or mulching. Avoid these when hoeing. If plants grow very tall stake them. Water in dry weather and feed when cobs near maturity. Cobs are ripe when the squeezed grain exudes rich and creamy (not pale and watery) liquid.
Pests and diseases	Corn smut turns kernels black; European corn borer and corn ear worm. Dust with insecticide.

Bulb and stalk vegetables

LEEK (*Allium porrum*). Although the leek is a member of the onion family it does not have the characteristic onion bulb but consists of a tightly packed sheaf of leaves, slightly bulbous at the base. The plant is usually blanched by earthing, which results in a cylindrical white base several inches long surmounted by thick, smooth, tapered green leaves. The flavour is milder than that of the onion.

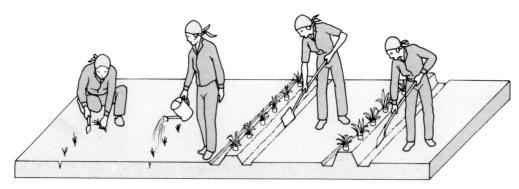

Seedlings can be planted in a slit (not hole) made by driving a trowel in about 5 in (12 cm). Place plant in slit with roots well down and fill slit with water which will fill it with soil. As plants grow they are earthed up to continue blanching. Leek may also be trenched like celery.

Leek
Musselburgh, Winter Crop, Mont Blanc.
Best soil
Rich and well composted.
Varieties
Early; mid-season; late.
Timetable
Germination 3 weeks. Maturing time 9 weeks for early, 11 weeks for later varieties.
How to sow
Under glass in March: in the open in April and May. Sow in ½ in (1 cm) drills, transplanting when about 6–8 in (15–20 cm) high about 6 in (15 cm) apart in rows 1 ft (30 cm) apart. Cut back roots to about 1½ in (3 cm) to facilitate planting.
Cultivation
Water well in summer; hoe regularly. As plants grow draw up soil to heighten blanching. In trench gradually return soil to trench for same purpose. When required lift with a fork. Leeks can winter in the allotment or garden.
Pests and diseases
Fairly free. To prevent onion fly sprinkle seedling rows with calomel dust. If white rot affects base of plants destroy those infected and avoid growing leeks there for several years.

ONION (*Allium cepa*). Widely cultivated in most countries, the onion is noteworthy for its strong taste and smell and contains a volatile oil that, when vaporised, affects the olfactory nerves causing tears. The onion is globe-shaped and is the swollen base of the stem. It is encased in a brittle, paper-like skin and the plant grows into tubular leaves. Small green onions harvested before the base has begun to swell are known as scallions in the United States, and spring onions in Britain.

SHALLOT (*Allium ascalonicum*). This is a type of onion but instead of a single bud the shallots grow in clusters, often flattish on one side. The inner skin has a purplish tinge. The shallot has a finer taste than the onion and is used for flavouring in cooking.

GARLIC (*Allium sativum*). A member of the onion family but its bulbs consist of a number of oily cloves held together by a fine papery skin. Garlic is used to flavour foods. Because of its highly pungent taste and smell it is usually used sparingly.

(1) onion; (2) shallot; (3) garlic.

Onion	Ailsa Craig, Bedforshire Champion, Autumn Queen, White Lisbon (salad), Small Paris Silverskin (pickling).
Best soil	Should have been dug and composted early in previous winter. Soil should be well raked and have a fine tilth.
Varieties	Flat-shaped or globe; shallots.
Timetable	Germination 3 weeks. Maturing time, spring-sown seeds 5½ months; late summer-sown 11½ months. Sets planted in March and April should mature from July to September.
How to sow	Sow seed in open in ½ in (1 cm) drills 1 ft (30 cm) apart. Thin to 2 in (5 cm) apart, then to 6 in (15 cm), using thinnings as spring onions. Remove unused thinnings, which attract onion fly. If planting glass-grown seedlings place base of bulb about ½ in (1 cm) below surface. If growing from sets push gently into soil 6 in (15 cm) apart with growing tip just showing.
Cultivation	Keep weed-free by hoeing or weeding by hand. Watch out for onion sets pushed up by frost and push them back into soil. Leaves falling over is a sign of the onion's maturity and bulbs can be lifted a fortnight or so later. Spread in sun to dry.
Pests and diseases	Onion fly produces small white maggots in bulb. Calomel dust sprinkled around seedlings when planted out can prevent.

Bulb and stalk vegetables

Preparing the onion bed
1 Dig in compost in the autumn. **2** Rake well. **3** Firm down in early spring for sowing or planting in April.

Sowing and planting
4 Onions can be sown in a seed box in a cold frame or greenhouse late in January. **5** Outdoors plant in drills in April and later in early September. **6** Seedlings are planted out in April after they have been hardened off in rows 1 ft (30 cm) apart.

Growing sets
Less troublesome than growing from seeds is to grow from sets, which are small, immature onions. If you grow from your own sets, cut back the dried leaves to close to the bulb. They are pressed into the soil 4 in (10 cm) apart in rows and soon begin to grow again.

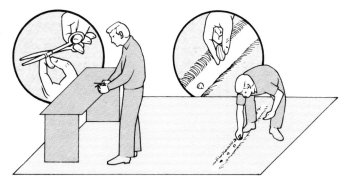

A good way to store onions is to make them up into ropes, and then hang them from the rafters in a cool, well-ventilated corner. Start with a loop made from 3 ft (1 m) of strong string or twine, and hang it from a nail. Then follow the diagrams.

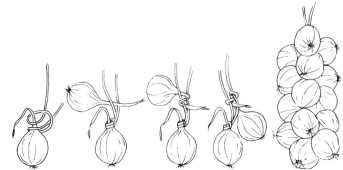

Cultivation

7 Dust plants with soot, if obtainable, or suitable insect deterrent. **8** Weeding is best done by hand to avoid disturbing the onion bulbs.

Harvesting

9 When the onions are mature the leaves will collapse. Maturing can be quickened in last stages by lifting bulbs slightly. Leave for a fortnight or so before harvesting. **10** After lifting with a fork or by hand, onions should be left in the sun to dry.

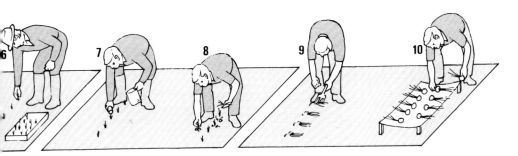

Growing garlic

Choose good cloves or segments from a garlic bulb. Plant them about 1 in (2 cm) deep in rows 1 ft (30 cm) apart in late February or early March. Pinch out flower heads. When foliage begins to turn yellow lift the bulbs and dry them, rubbing off loose skin and dead leaves.

Growing shallots

Choose a sunny position. Plant bulbs with their tips at soil level in February or March. Each bulb produces a cluster of up to a dozen similar bulbs, which will be ready by July or August. As clusters develop draw soil lightly away from them.

Bulb and stalk vegetables

CELERY (*Apium graveolens*). This vegetable is grown for its crisp but succulent leaf stalk, which is often blanched by earthing in soil or wrapping the stems to prevent chlorophyll (green pigment) from forming. The plants grow to about 2 ft (60 cm) in height and the leaf stems are tightly packed with toothed leaves at the tip. Celery can be cooked but is more often eaten raw.

In April prepare a trench about 15 in (37 cm) deep and 15 in (37 cm) wide. Fork over the bottom soil, lay on a generous layer of compost or manure, tread down and cover with 3–4 in (7–10 cm) of soil. Earth removed from the trench should be banked up for further use.

Celery

Trench: Giant White, Giant Pink, Giant Red, Prizetaker.
Self-blanching. Golden Self, American Green, Utah.

Best soil

Well-prepared trench in sunny position, for ordinary variety; well-dug manured soil for self-blanching.

Varieties

Trench, usually white but may be pink or reddish, late maturing; self-blanching, yellow or green, early maturing.

Timetable

Germination 2 to 4 weeks. Maturing time 7 months. Self-blanching seedlings planted in May or June will be ready between August and October; trench varieties from October onwards.

How to sow

In heat under glass during March in shallow drills in seed boxes. Plant out in May or June. If you do not have glass, buy seedlings from a nurseryman.

Cultivation

As above. Protect seedlings from slugs. Remove side shoots or suckers before earthing up. Dust leaves with old soot. Water regularly.

Pests and diseases

Celery fly may produce brown blisters on leaves, which should be removed. Soot (see Cultivation) helps prevent celery fly.

When plants are about 4 in (10 cm) high and have been hardened off they should be planted in the trench about 9 in (22 cm) apart. If the trench is made a few inches wider, a double row can be planted. When about 10 in (25 cm) high, tie the stems just below the leaves and begin to return the earth to blanch the stems, continuing as plants grow.

Self-Blanching
The self-blanching variety need no trenching or earthing up. Seedlings should be planted about 8 in (20 cm) apart in a square. As they grow the light is excluded, thus helping blanching. Boards around, making an open box, blanch the outside plants.

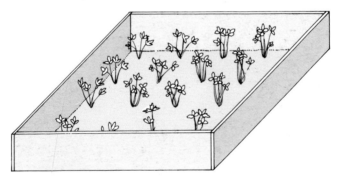

Harvesting
To harvest, lift as required, working down the trench. Lift carefully, clearing one side before levering out with a spade.

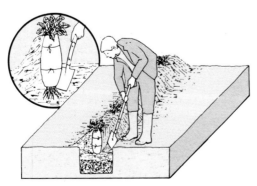

Bulb and stalk vegetables

RHUBARB (*Rheum rhaponticum*). Although rhubarb is a vegetable its pinkish-red fleshy stalks are used like a fruit, cooked in desserts and jams. The stalks grow from a bulky root crown and each is tipped by a single large, dark green crinkled leaf. These because they contain oxalic acid, are dangerous for human consumption. Rhubarb is also used medicinally.

To force rhubarb outdoors, put a box or a bucket over each crown, and surround these with straw. If this is done around the middle of January, you should be able to pull the rhubarb up to three weeks early. Do not force the same plants each year. The plants respond better if clumps are lifted and exposed to frost for 2 weeks (not in wet weather).

Rhubarb
Champagne early, Victoria, Holstein Blood red
Best soil
Well dug, heavyish soil containing plenty of humus.
Varieties
Early and late.
Timetable
By forcing, sticks may be pulled from February until June.
How to sow
The quickest way is to plant sections of a crown, because plants grown from seed take nearly two years to bear. Plant roots 3 ft (1 m) apart, just covering buds. Add bonemeal to topsoil.
Cultivation
No sticks should be pulled until the roots have been in the ground for a whole season. Early outdoor rhubarb can be forced by putting an old bucket or carton over the crown. Never cut rhubarb sticks; always pull them from the crown. Remember that the leaves are poisonous.

Rhubarb
Plant new crowns in early November. If you have rhubarb already established, lift some of the crowns and leave on top of the soil, replanting in late January or February. Don't worry about frost.

SEAKALE (*Crambe maritima*). This vegetable gets its name from the fact that it originated near the seashore. Because of this, salt is required in the soil and seaweed makes an ideal manure. The vegetable is grown for its sweet, succulent stems, which can be eaten raw like celery or cooked. Growing from seed is a lengthy business taking two years and it is best to plant 'thongs' or roots, which are planted in a specially prepared bed 15 in (37 cm) apart in rows 15 in (37 cm) apart. In late October the foliage is cut off, and the roots lifted and moved indoors or into a shed; there they can be forced to produce shoots, which can be cut when 7–8 in (17–20 cm) long.

ASPARAGUS (*Asparagus officinalis*). A member of the lily family, asparagus is regarded as an aristocrat among vegetables. The part that is cooked and eaten is the young shoot or stem, which is cut off close to the ground when it stands about 6–8 in (15–20 cm) high. If allowed to grow it resembles a small tree with fern-like leaves (used by florists). Asparagus is planted or sown on specially prepared beds and is not harvested until the third year but then continues to produce for many years. The asparagus bed should be well drained, weed-free and well matured, and in a sunny position. The vegetable can be grown from seed but planting one- or two-year-old plants is easier. They are best planted in trenches about 1 ft (30 cm) wide and 9 in (22 cm) deep with manure in the bottom. Do not harvest the shoots until the third year.

Bulb and stalk vegetables

CHICORY (*Cichorium intybus*). This is a winter salad vegetable grown for its forced chicons or shoots. These consist of tightly packed leaves, which grow flame-shaped and are blanched. The plant is grown out of doors, but the long, milky roots are dug up in November to be taken indoors or put in a shed, forced in the dark.

Sow in early June in rows 18 in (45 cm) apart, thinning the plants to 9 in (22 cm) apart. The soil should be well manured or composted and deeply dug, as the roots are long. When the foliage has died down, in November, remove it, dig up the roots and trim off any side-shoots. Plant roots close together in a deep box with about 6 in (15 cm) of compost covered by the same depth of fine soil. They should be well watered and covered to keep out light. Within about 3 weeks the pale chicons will be 7–8 in (17–20 cm) high and are ready for harvesting. Within a month there should be a second crop.

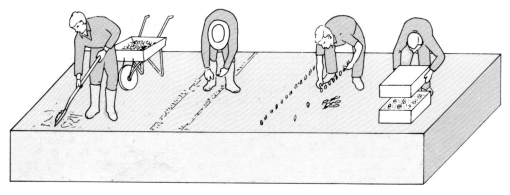

ARTICHOKE (GLOBE) (*Cynara scolymus*). Grey-green in colour, the artichoke plant grows to a height of about 3 ft (1 m). It has large, prickly leaves and resembles the thistle. It is cultivated for its edible flower heads, which have thick, green, solidly packed petals, the bases of which are succulent. It likes a light, well-drained, well-manured soil. It is best grown by planting secondary shoots 4 in (10 cm) deep and 3 ft (1 m) apart. Harvest when flower scales are about to open.

CARDOON (*Cynara scolymus*). This vegetable belongs to the globe artichoke family, but it is grown not for its edible flowers but for its stems, or chards, which are blanched like celery. Indeed cardoons are grown in the same way as celery in well-manured trenches. Seeds can be sown direct in the trenches in May, or planted out if seedlings have been brought on under glass. Blanching should be started in September and the cardoons should be ready from November on.

FINOCCHIO (*Foeniculum dulce*). Although this is often known as 'Florence fennel' it should not be confused with the herb fennel (page 107). It is grown for its swollen stem base, which is used either raw in salads or cooked. Its leaves have an aniseed flavour and can be used in sauces and soups. It likes rich, moist soil in a sunny position and can be grown from seed sown in shallow drills 18 in (45 cm) apart, thinning out to about 8 in (20 cm). As the stems swell they should be earthed up to blanch and should be copiously watered to encourage swelling. Lift stems when they are tennis-ball size.

Vegetable fruits

Tomatoes love warmth so choose a sunny spot – against a wall or fence if you are lucky enough to have one.

TOMATO (*Lycopersicum esculentum*). One of the most popular of the fruit vegetables, the tomato is in fact a berry. The plant grows to a height of several feet and is usually staked for support, but bush varieties do not need this. In the standard variety the fruits grow in trusses from the main stem. The flower is yellow and the unripe fruit is round, smooth and green, becoming eventually a rich red. The tomato is often grown under glass or at least has to be ripened indoors, but given good weather it can not only be successfully grown outdoors but will even ripen in the open.

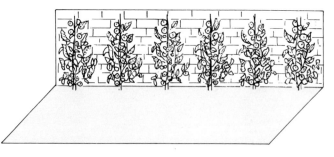

Tomato	*Outdoor*: Market King, Gardener's Delight (standards), French Cross (bush). *Greenhouse*: Moneymaker, Alicante, Super Cross.
Best soil	Well dug and composted or manured. Apply fertiliser before planting.
Varieties	Standard, which need support; bush and dwarf, which don't.
Timetable	March and April sowing under glass should be ready for planting out in late May, with harvesting in August and September.
How to sow	Under glass, planting seedlings outdoors when about 8 in (20 cm) high. Or buy sturdy plants from a nurseryman, planting out about 18 in (45 cm) apart in rows 2½ ft (75 cm) apart.
Cultivation	Support standard varieties by tying stem to a 5 ft (1.5 m) cane. Nip out side shoots, which appear where leaf stalk joins stem. Remove yellowing leaves. When four trusses of tomatoes have set, pinch out the main growing point to stop further growth. Keep plants well watered and feed with liquid manure when tomatoes have set. Bush and dwarf varieties grow naturally and need no cultivation but put straw on ground to protect low-growing fruit.
Pests and diseases	Split fruit is caused by excessive watering of very dry soil. Tomatoes can be affected by potato blight, which causes decaying patches on fruit: spray with copper fungicide.

Getting fresh
When picking tomatoes leave the calyx attached, not only for the appearance but because it helps the fruit to remain fresh.

Standards
Plant out seedlings when 8 in (20 cm) high and tie to 5 ft (1.5 m) canes. Nip out side shoots between stem and leaf stalk when 1 in (2 cm) long (inset). Nip off growing point of plant, two leaves above fourth truss of tomatoes, after fruit has formed.

Bush varieties that grow to 1–2½ ft (30–75 cm) high can be cultivated under cloches. No support or nipping out required. Tomatoes that do not ripen on plant can be ripened on windowsills (ripe tomatoes encourage green ones) or in drawers or cupboards.

It's in the bag
You can buy polythene bags filled with specially prepared compost and plant and grow your tomatoes in the bag itself. Tomatoes can also be grown outdoors in 9–12 in (22–30 cm) pots using compost and watering and feeding regularly.

Vegetable fruits

Greenhouse technique
You can use your greenhouse for producing seedlings both for planting outdoors and for growing in the greenhouse for the full season. How you grow them in the greenhouse depends on its size. They can be grown in a good soil bed; in pots; or by ring culture.

Tomatoes under glass
In unheated houses sow in March to plant out at the end of April and harvest in July. In heated houses sow in December to be planted out in the following March. Sow in boxes of compost 1 in (2 cm) apart, and cover with polythene, keeping temperature at 60–65°F (16–18°C). On germination remove polythene and place box in well-lit part of greenhouse. Move to 3 in (7 cm) pots when leaves have formed and keep in temperature of 50–55°F (10–13°C).

When the seedlings are about 8 in (20 cm) high, dark green and sturdy, they can be planted in 12 in (30 cm) pots, in the soil bed, or outdoors. Those remaining indoors are treated similarly to those grown outdoors (i.e. stakes and side shoots pinched out) but they need not be 'stopped' until the plant has reached the roof of the greenhouse.

When the trusses form it is a good thing to spray the plants or tap the supports to help pollination; and when the fruit has set feed with liquid manure. Soil should always be kept moist, especially if growing in pots or pre-packed bags.

In ring culture the seedlings are planted out in bottomless rings filled with special tomato compost, which are placed on a bed of ashes or sand. The compost in the ring is kept fed by liquid fertiliser and the base is constantly watered to keep it moist. The plants' roots feed from the compost and drink from the base.

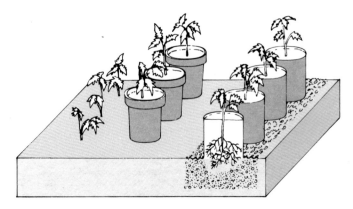

1 soil bed
2 in pots
3 ring cultures

MARROW (*Cucurbita ovifera*). The bush or trailing plant produces large green or yellowish-green fruits, a large part of which consists of water. They are used as a vegetable or for making jam and can be stuffed with meat and baked. The trailing varieties occupy a good deal of space and are best trained on a tripod. A small variety of the marrow is the courgette.

Trailing varieties take up lots of room so it is best to cultivate them around a tripod or trellis.

Marking time
Amaze the family by secretly scratching your children's names lightly on baby marrows. The scar will grow with the marrow and delight them when brought in from the allotment.

Boosting marrows
Bury a flower pot alongside your marrow plants. Keep filled with water and you will amaze your friends – even more so if you thread a woollen wick through the stems down into the jar. But that's cheating.

Marrow
Bush: Green Bush, White Bush, *Trailing*: Long White and Long Green.
Best soil
As for cucumber, well composted in a protected sunny position.
Varieties
Bush; trailing; courgettes.
Timetable
Sow in May out of doors for harvesting in August and September. Germination time about 1 week. Maturing time 2½ to 3½ months.
How to sow
As for cucumber, by preparing special small pits filled with compost and soil. Sow 3 or 4 seeds, placing seeds edge downwards in soil. Retain strongest seedling. Or seedlings can be brought on under glass. Scatter slug pellets.
Cultivation
Marrows require plenty of water. Sink a flower pot in the ground beside the plant and fill with water regularly. Help pollination by inserting male flower into female. Main shoots of trailing variety should be stopped when 2–3 ft (60–95 cm) long. Store in winter hung in nets.
Pests and diseases
Marrows can suffer from cucumber mosaic virus. This mottles leaves, retards growth. Destroy affected plants.

Vegetable fruits

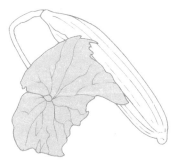

CUCUMBER (*Cucumis sativus*). This is a trailing vine with a dark green fruit up to 2 ft (60 cm) long and 2 in (5 cm) in diameter. The seeds form a core surrounded by a pale green watery pulp; the crisp cucumber is much used in salads. Those grown outdoors are called ridge cucumbers, those grown in frames or greenhouses frame cucumbers. Outdoor cucumbers need a protected spot in the sun.

Outdoor cucumbers at best grown in specially prepared pits about 1 ft³ (30 cm³) in size, filled with soil and compost; and surface fertiliser.

Cucumber	*Outdoor*: Baton Vert, Nadir, Perfection, Kyoto (climbing) *Underglass*: Conqueror, Telegraph improved.
Best soil	Very rich and well drained.
Varieties	Ordinary rough-skinned; F_1 Hybrid; Japanese smooth-skinned.
Timetable	Sow under glass in April for planting out in June, or outdoors in late May or early June. Germination time 7 to 9 days. Maturing period 2½ to 3½ months.
How to sow	Under glass in pots to produce seedlings. Or sow three or four seeds in the centre of each prepared pit, later removing weaker seedlings leaving the strongest one. When grown under glass, plant out in pits after hardening off.
Cultivation	When two pairs of leaves have developed, the growing point should be stopped (pinched out) to help produce side shoots. These in turn should be stopped when they have produced one fruit or no fruit. If the plant is allowed to trail put straw under fruit. Or the plant can be tied to grow up a wire frame. Keep soil moist. Mulching helps during growth.
Pests and diseases	Syringe with water to prevent red spider mite. If affected, burn mottled leaves. Spray with insecticide against greenfly, which spread cucumber mosaic virus.

SWEET PEPPER

(*Capsicum annuum*). Red peppers picked while unripe are called green peppers. The fruit somewhat resembles a large flat-sided tomato and is often used chopped or sliced in salads. In mild conditions peppers can be grown out of doors under cloches, which can be removed when the plant grows too tall. Seedlings should be started off in a propagating frame in March and transplanted into pots before hardening off for planting out in May or June. Plants should be 18 in (45 cm) apart in composted soil in a sunny situation and the soil should be kept moist. When the fruit begins to swell, water well and feed with liquid manure.

COURGETTE (*Cucurbita*).

These are ordinary marrows that are gathered while still young and tender. They are planted 20 in (50 cm) apart, and should be kept well watered. Cloches are often used to give them a good start. Take precautions against slugs. When the plants fruit, pick them while they are still small. If they are left on the plant and continue to grow, the flavour will be spoiled and the plant will produce less fruits. Courgettes may be cooked whole, or larger ones can be sliced.

PUMPKIN (*Cucurbita pepo*).

Not many gardeners grow this heavyweight of the vegetable world, but if you have American friends and want to give them traditional pumpkin pie on Thanksgiving Day all you need to remember is that the pumpkin is a member of the marrow family and is cultivated in the same way as trailing marrows. Sow in mid-May 4 ft (1.2 m) apart, sowing three seeds at each point and thinning seedlings to the strongest one. The soil should be well manured as for marrows.

AUBERGINE (*Solanum melongena ovigerum*).

This plant is closely related to the potato, but is grown not for its tubers but for the large swollen berries, usually purple in colour. They have a delicious flavour and are usually sliced and cooked in oil as a vegetable. The aubergine is often called the egg-plant from the shape of its purple fruit. Aubergines are generally grown in greenhouses from seed sown in January but they can be grown in the open in mild conditions, planted out 15 in (37 cm) apart in June. They require well-manured soil and plenty of sun and water. The fruits should be harvested when not too big and when they are well-coloured and shiny.

Herbs

For our purpose, herbs are those plants whose stems and leaves can be used for flavouring foods, and which can be grown in the allotment or vegetable garden. Of these we have selected a dozen or so of the commonest and most useful. There are dozens of other herbs grown for other purposes than flavouring food – for instance, for their scent or medicinal value – but few gardeners can afford the space to grow them all.

The traditional herb gardens of the great houses were laid out almost like carpet gardens, the low-growing herbs with their delicately tinted blossoms and variegated leaves mingling in a colourful array made even more agreeable by the scent of aromatic foliage. Our average gardener, however, will certainly have to be satisfied with a lot less than this. He may set aside a small section of his plot as a miniature herb garden, or may decide to grow individual herbs wherever he can spare the space. You don't have to grow your herbs all together and

CHIVES (*Allium schoenoprasum*). A perennial onion-like plant, which grows up to 9 in (22 cm) in height on well-drained sites. Its tubular leaves are used to give a mild onion flavour to salads and other dishes. They can be cut down to soil level in the spring to encourage further growth. Flowers appearing in May and June should be removed immediately.

CHERVIL (*Anthriscus cerefolium*). Flourishes in well-drained soil not too exposed to the sun. It grows to about 18 in (45 cm) high. Sow at intervals in spring and summer, thinning to 1 ft (30 cm) apart. Pinch out white flowers when they appear. The fern-like leaves, smelling faintly of parsley, are used in soups and in omelettes *fines herbes*. It is an annual.

TARRAGON (*Artemisia dracunculus*). Plant in spring or autumn about 9 in (22 cm) apart. It grows to over 18 in (45 cm) in height. The dark green leaves should be picked before the green-white flowers appear in high summer. Finely chopped, they are used with chervil in *fines herbes* and to give a distinctive flavour to sauces and to roast chicken. Perennial.

BORAGE (*Borago officinalis*). This hardy annual reaches 2–3 ft (60–95 cm) high and has hairy, silver-green leaves and bright blue flowers (beloved by bees). Its young leaves (2 months), when crushed, are used to flavour summer drinks (such as Pimms), and the flowers can be crystallised. Sow in April or September sparingly and thin to 1 ft (30 cm) apart. Although an annual, borage self-seeds prolifically.

there are positive advantages in planting such shrubs as rosemary and bay, which grow to a height of more than 6 ft (2 m), in selected individual sites, perhaps against a fence or in a border.

Nearly all herbs do well on well-drained light soil, and all are sun-lovers. Generally they are fairly free from pests and disease and, apart from keeping them free of weeds, are not very demanding on the gardener's time.

HORSERADISH (*Cochlearia armoracia*). The roots of this perennial, 1–1½ in (2–3 cm) thick, have a hot, pungent flavour and are used, grated with vinegar or cream, as a relish. It requires little or no cultivation and is best grown in a corner of the allotment. The roots are planted about 2 in (5 cm) deep in February and only a few plants, 18 in (45 cm) apart, are needed. Harvest in summer, storing the roots in sand during the winter.

FENNEL (*Foeniculum vulgare*). Sow in March, thinning to 2 ft (60 cm) apart, for fennel can grow to over 6 ft (2 m). Its fine, bluish-green leaves, like those of dill, have an aniseed flavour; and, also like dill, its dried seeds are used in pickling vinegar. Fennel is a perennial.

BAY (*Laurus nobilis*). An evergreen shrub that can grow to over 10 ft (3 m) if not trimmed. Its dark green leaves provide a strong flavour to many dishes, and a bay leaf – with a sprig of parsley and of thyme – is essential in a *bouquet garni*. Leaves can be used fresh or dried. Grown from cuttings taken in August or September, kept in a cold frame and planted out in early spring or the following autumn. Likes well-drained soil and shelter from cold winds.

MINT (*Mentha spicata*). This perennial grows 12–20 in (30–50 cm) high in dampish soil. Plant cuttings between October and April. Has a vigorous rooting system and spreads widely unless controlled. Its characteristically fragrant leaves are used in mint sauce and for flavouring vegetables and summer drinks.

APPLEMINT (*Mentha rotundifolia*). This species has more rounded leaves and a rather more subtle flavour but grows in much the same way.
1 Mint
2 Applemint

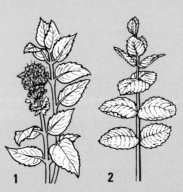

Herbs

Gather herbs on a dry, sunny morning. Where it is the leaves and stems that are used, they should be harvested when young and tender. Where it is the flowers that are used, they should be in full bloom. When picking stems and leaves try not to bruise the leaves. Dead or blemished leaves should be discarded. Dirty leaves should be washed gently in cool water.

Lay the herbs on flat trays, keeping them well separated to conserve individual aromas. Leave in warm and dry conditions, such as an airing cupboard, for a week or so, turning the herbs daily until they are brittle. Then put them temporarily in glass jars to test whether moisture remains — if it does, it will show on the inside of the glass. If there is still moisture, renew the drying process.

Then remove leaves from stem and store them, crumbled, in a labelled airtight container. If the containers are translucent they should be kept from direct light. Herbs with small leaves can be dried by tying them in bundles and

MARJORAM (*Origanum marjorana*). A small shrub reaching 2 ft (60 cm) in height. Can be grown from seed under glass and planted out in May. Likes a well-drained, sunny site. Its grey-green, aromatic leaves are used, fresh or dried, in flavouring soups, stews etc, and are often used as a substitute for thyme. Bears pale lilac flowers in the summer.

BASIL (*Ocimum basilicum*). A half-hardy annual, which prefers a well-drained fertile soil in a sunny position. Sow outdoors in mid-May. Grows to about 2 ft (60 cm) in height with pale green leaves smelling faintly of cloves. Bears small white flowers in August. The leaves, used to flavour many foods and sauces, are best when young.

PARSLEY (*Petroselinum crispum*). A favourite herb for flavouring and garnishing. Likes a well-drained site in the sun. Sow in the open in ½ in (1 cm) drills in February or March, and in high summer for a winter or spring supply. Thin to 8 in (20 cm) apart. Germination is particularly slow so don't lose heart. Remove young flowering stems in summer to encourage further growth.

DILL (*Peucedanum graveolens*). Sow in March or April, thinning out to 9 in (22 cm) apart. Grows to about 3 ft (1 m). The leaves, which have a slight aniseed flavour, can be used with fish and sauces, the dried seeds in pickling vinegar.

hanging them upside down in cool, airy conditions. These herbs are best stored whole and not crumbled until you are ready to use them. In this way they keep their aroma well. When using herbs, don't forget that dried herbs have a far stronger flavour than fresh ones.

Some herbs, such as chives, parsley and chervil, do not dry well and are best used fresh, although some can be frozen. If herbs such as fennel and dill are grown for their seeds, the stems should be picked when the seeds are ripe, placed in trays and left to dry. The seeds can then be removed and left to dry.

ROSEMARY (*Rosmarinus officinalis*). An evergreen shrub about 6 ft (2 m) high, which flourishes in well-drained soil and likes the sun. Has small narrow leaves much paler underneath than on top. They have a sweet, lingering perfume and are used fresh or dried in cooking. Usually grown from cuttings, spaced 2–3 ft (60–95 cm) apart. Bears lilac-coloured flowers in May.

SAGE (*Salvia officinalis*). This evergreen shrub, growing up to 2 ft (60 cm) in height, is recognised by its furry, grey-green, highly aromatic leaves and purple or white flowers (June and July). Prefers sunny, well-drained soil. Can be grown from seeds or cuttings (planted March or September), spaced 15 in (37 cm) apart. The strongly tasting leaves (picked in May and again in August) are used for flavouring meat dishes.

THYME (*Thymus vulgaris*). One of the most useful of herbs, used to flavour many dishes and an essential ingredient – with a sprig of parsley and a bay leaf – of a *bouquet garni*. Can be sown or grown from cuttings planted out in September. Cuttings can be taken in May or June and planted in potting compost. Bears lilac flowers during summer months.

'Only an honest man can grow parsley'
That's what country folk say, but parsley takes a long time to germinate – 4 to 6 weeks. A good tip is to sow a row of radishes (which grow quickly) in with the parsley. They mark the row for you and will have matured and can be pulled by the time the parsley shows.

Friend or foe No.1

'Keep well watered' must be an infuriating instruction to the allotment holder who has no water supply or very little. If nature fails you, remember that it is usually better not to start watering than to start and then have to stop. And don't forget that the more humus you can dig into your soil, in one form or another, the longer the soil will remain moist.

If the reverse is the case and your plot is liable to become excessively wet the remedy may lie in double-digging or drainage. Dig a hole at the lowest part of your allotment. If at the end of a week there is water at the bottom, you may need to double-dig. If the hole is part filled, then some form of drainage is probably needed.

First a word of warning! The gardener, presented as he is here with a solid array of enemies, could be forgiven for thinking of surrendering without a struggle. But he might well do the same if he were confronted with all the illnesses to which man is subject, all at the same time. He should take comfort from the fact that some of the horrors here described may never come his way, and they are certainly unlikely to come all together.

Also he should remember that he has friends as well as enemies. New disease-resistant varieties are constantly being developed. Even the birds that attack his seedlings also eat the insects that attack them in other ways. And not all insects are harmful. Ladybirds, for example, eat greenfly: bees pollinate the plants. Even the weather can be friend or foe. A frost at the wrong time can cause havoc, as can a protracted drought or spell of wet weather. But a good spell at the right time can work miracles.

It is important to know how to distinguish the good from the bad: how to identify pests from the damage they have done and how to diagnose the disease from the evidence and how to deal with it. Methods range from such simple devices as growing carrots and onions next to each other (because the fly that attacks each dislikes the smell of the other plant), to spraying with the latest sophisticated chemicals.

And there is the soil itself, the matter of ensuring the right balance, the right moisture content and the right degree of fertility. All are related problems and most do not have a difficult solution.

Slugs and snails, nocturnal raiders, are omnivorous eaters of the tender seedlings and of the leaves and stems of older plants. They live under rubbish so keep your garden tidy and clean; scatter pellets around seed rows, especially if you see their shiny trails and other signs of marauding.

The slow-moving, dark-coloured millipede can play havoc with seedlings and the root systems of older plants, as can the woodlouse. Incidentally they both curl up (perhaps with shame) if disturbed. Like slugs, woodlice live under rubbish, so keep your plot clean and tidy. Ants can be a nuisance, dislodging soil around roots and carrying infection.

The sluggish, dark grey leatherjacket, the quicker-moving wireworm and the slower cutworm are all underground pests. The first two devour roots and the orange-coloured wireworm is a real bore, making holes in potatoes and other root crops. The cutworm, a large caterpillar, either grey or brown, cuts through the stems of cabbages and lettuces at soil level.

Not all subterranean activists are enemies of the gardener. The ubiquitous earthworm is very much his friend and should never be discouraged. It burrows through the earth creating air holes that help the earth to retain air and moisture. As it burrows, its castings build up the topsoil on which the gardener relies.

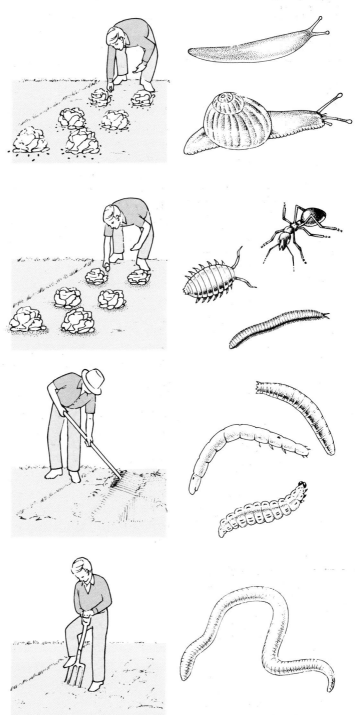

Friend or foe No.2

Rhubarb leaves
These contain oxalic acid and are poisonous so don't cook and eat them. But you need not waste them. Why not poison a few aphids instead of yourself? Chop up 4 lb (1.8 kg) of the leaves, boil in ½ gall (2.3 l) of water for 30 minutes and strain off the liquid. Add 1¼ oz (35 g) of soap flakes when cool and spray it over aphis-infested plants.

Some precautions that can be taken against disease and depredation are dusting seed rows with appropriate powders and repeating when planting out; protecting seedlings with slug pellets scattered on the soil; spraying to kill insects infesting plants and to discourage their attacks; digging and raking in plant foods and using liquid feed to make up deficiencies. Above all remember not to leave diseased plants you have pulled up lying around, and not to put them in the compost – a sure way to spread the disease later. The bonfire is the only place for them, roots and all.

Like human beings, plants can be attacked by infectious diseases. These may be caused not by insects or other pests but by such things as viruses, bad drainage, impurities or deficiencies in the soil, or even bad sowing and growing methods.

The fact that a plant is sick, because it is diseased or has been attacked by a pest of one sort or another, is evident in much the same way as with a human being. The plant may be 'off-colour' in the strictest sense of the word, for its leaves may turn brown or white or develop a mould for no apparent reason. And, again like a human being, a plant may become listless and droopy, and in the end collapse. The gardener quickly develops a recognition of symptoms such as leaves losing their gloss, even if he cannot immediately diagnose the disease.

As with humans, sickness often develops from dietary faults. Leaf scorch in potatoes may be due to a deficiency of potash in the soil, and potato scab may result from an excess of lime. The important thing is to spot and identify the ailment in its early stages and to take the necessary steps while they can be effective. In the case of some diseases there may be nothing to do but destroy the affected plant and avoid growing that particular crop in that part of your allotment for a long time – probably for years.

Don't forget that diseases may be caused by infection, and the infection remains not only in the soil, but in pots and seedboxes, which is why they should always be cleaned between periods of use. Some diseases and pests must be reported to the authorities.

Familiar diseases affecting leaves: potato and tomato blight produces brown patches on leaves; downy mildew affects brassicas, leeks and onions, and discolours their leaves with a sort of mould; pea mildew leaves a white powder on pea leaves; and tomato leaf mould causes yellow blotches, purple underneath, on tomato leaves.

Common pests that attack vegetable leaves and fruit: the cabbage caterpillar eats large holes in the leaves of brassicas; the maggot of the pea moth burrows into peas; the leaf miner lays eggs in celery leaves, raising white blisters; blackfly attack broad beans and beetroot; greenfly attack brassicas; thrips distort the pods of peas and beans; slugs and snails eat almost anything tender that gets in their way.

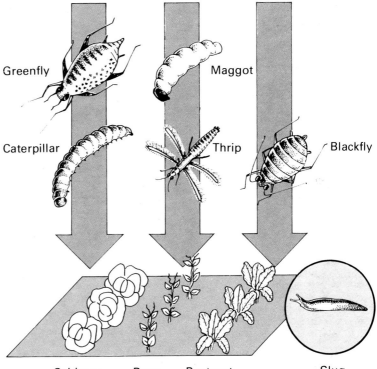

Greenfly
Maggot
Caterpillar
Thrip
Blackfly

Cabbage   Peas   Beetroot
Slug

1 Potato blight
2 Club root
3 Wireworms, leatherjackets, Millipedes, chafer grubs
4 Carrot and onion fly
5 Cutworm

Some pests and diseases of roots: potato blight causes soft patches on tubers; club root swells the roots of brassicas, eventually killing the plant; wireworms, leatherjackets, millipedes and chafer grubs bore into roots and tubers; carrot and onion fly lay eggs in the roots; the cutworm eats through the stems of brassicas and lettuces at soil level.

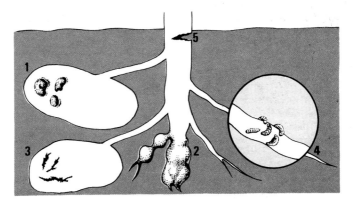

Chapter four
Fruits
of your labour

An allotment is not an orchard. In any case
some fruit trees take years to mature and bear
and an allotment holder should be certain of a
long tenancy before planting such trees as
apple, pear or plum. Soft fruit such as
raspberries, gooseberries, currants and
strawberries are a different matter. They mature
more quickly, and neither grow to the height of
the others nor put out the same demanding
roots. If you do decide to grow apples it may be
best to think of training your trees along wires
in cordons or espaliered. This is economical in
space, attractive in appearance and less likely to
cause annoyance to your neighbours than
standard trees.

A large fruited perpetual
strawberry (St Joseph) from
a 19th century seed
catalogue

This chapter tells you not only how to plant your trees etc, but also how to prune them in order to produce the best fruit. Some demand considerable care. It also tells you how to harvest and where possible store fruit – those that are bottled or boxed and those that can be frozen.

The most popular soft fruits are strawberries, raspberries, gooseberries and the three varieties of currants: black, red and white. There are others, such as loganberries and cultivated blackberries. All of them can be grown without great difficulty and often catch crops such as lettuce can be grown between rows to save space.

Strawberries are rather a special case. They are more demanding on plant food, require more constant care and take rather more space. But few would say that they are not worth it.

Training fruit

Where you grow your fruit depends very much on the sort of fruit and the size of your allotment or garden. If there is a wall in the latter then you could certainly use the cordon or espalier method as described on the opposite page. These methods can be used for gooseberries and currants as well as for apples and pears. Soft fruits should be from about 2 ft (60 cm) or more apart, in rows 5 ft (1.5 m) apart, so a fair amount of space is taken up; but even if you are not cordoning they can be grown as bushes along your boundaries. You will need to protect soft fruits with plastic netting from the ravages of birds as the fruit ripens. The height of luxury, of course, is a fruit cage high enough for you to work inside.

Trees company
When buying fruit trees do make sure whether they are self-fertilising or cross-pollinating. If the latter you will need to plant another appropriate variety of apple nearby to ensure pollination. Your nurseryman will advise you.

Avoid planting fruit trees in winter: early November is best. Dig a hole 2 ft (60 cm) deep and about 4 ft (1.2 m) square. Drive in a stake to support the young tree. After forking the subsoil make a small mound in the centre of the hole, over which you spread out the roots (which then slope downwards). Gradually fill in the hole, firming down well as you go along. When planting is finished the soil should be level with the soil mark on the stem of the tree. Attach the supporting stake to the tree by wire or strong twine, being sure to wrap some cloth or a piece of old inner tubing round the stem to prevent cutting into the bark.

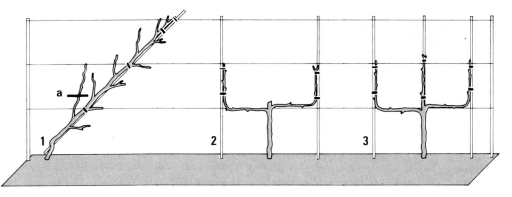

Above are the processes in training trees in single, double and triple cordons. **(1)** The 'maiden' tree is allowed to grow. Lateral branches are pruned back (**a**) every summer to about 6 in (15 cm) from stem. When tree has reached the desired height the stem is cut back. Laterals are pruned back every summer to about 6 in (15 cm) forming a single cordon. **(2)** For double cordons cut the tree's stem back to about 1 ft (30 cm) where two buds face in opposite directions. In summer tie the two grown shoots horizontally along wire, and when they are about 7 in (17 cm) long train them upwards on canes. Cut back side shoots in November to two buds forming fruiting spurs. **(3)** For triple cordons as for double, but the stem is cut where there is also an upward-growing bud. The central shoot that develops is trained up a cane parallel with the others. All three are pruned as with a double cordon.

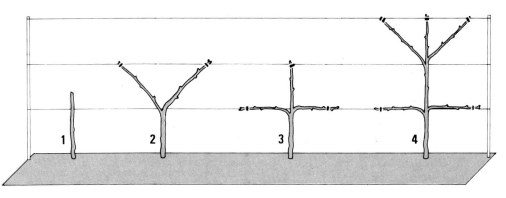

To espalier: **(1)** Cut back the maiden about 15 in (37 cm) from soil level. **(2)** Treat as for triple cordon but train side branches for the first summer at 45° to next wire. **(3)** Then bring them back to lie horizontally on bottom wire, i.e. about 1 ft (30 cm) above soil. **(4)** Cut back centre stem to about 2 ft (60 cm) after first year and repeat process until desired height is reached. Side branches should be cut back by about half a season's growth and shoots cut back in summer to about 5 in (12 cm).

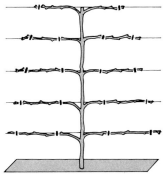

Soft fruits

Raspberries and strawberries are the most popular soft fruits. Raspberries grow tall on canes and need support; strawberries lie on the soil, from which the fruit must be protected. Strawberries ripen from June to September depending on the variety; raspberries can be picked from July onwards and some are specially bred for fruiting in autumn. Both like well-manured and composted soil, but strawberries dislike an excess of lime. Both are

Stages in growing strawberries

Strawberries are usually planted out in early autumn in a prepared bed that has been well manured and composted. **(1)** Plants should be about 15–18 in (37–45 cm) apart, in rows 2–2½ ft (60–75 cm) apart. **(2)** A good plan is to build a small mound in the centre of the planting hole so that roots can spread down and out. Crowns must be level with the soil surface. **(3)** Water after planting out. **(4)** Keep bed clean by hoeing gently. **(5)** Give top dressing of general fertiliser in February or March. **(6)** Cut out runners as they develop (unless you want to propagate them). **(7)** Net bed as protection against birds. **(8)** Put straw or straw mats under fruit to protect from soil and slugs.

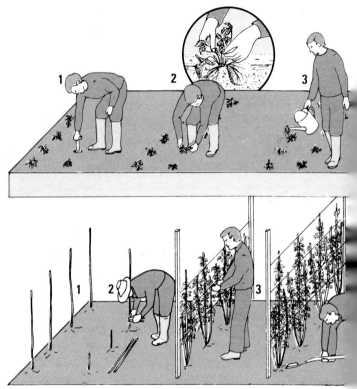

Stages in growing raspberries

(1) Plant out canes in autumn about 2 ft (60 cm) apart; rows should be about 6 ft (2 m) apart; plant about 3 in (7 cm) deep. **(2)** After firming down soil cut down canes to about 9 in (22 cm). **(3)** Tie canes to wires as they grow. **(4)** Dress soil with sulphate of potash in late winter or early spring and with top dressing of general fertiliser in spring. **(5)** Cut back tops of canes to about 5 ft (1.5 m) in early spring. **(6)** Cover with nylon netting or old lace curtain. **(7)** After harvesting fruit remove all

grown initially from canes or plants but can be propagated from raspberry cane cuttings or from the runners thrown out by your own strawberry plants. (See pages 120 and 122 for further details.)

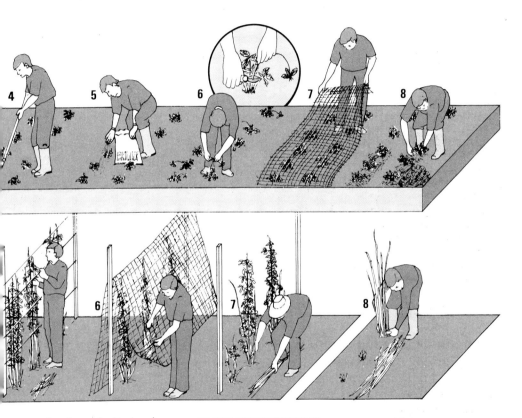

canes that have fruited or in excess of 6–8 of the strongest new canes. **(8)** Autumn-fruiting varieties are left unpruned until the following spring, when they are cut down to just above soil level.

Firm footing
A good way to counteract the pull on the uprights carrying your wires is to fix 9 in (22 cm) battens 18 in (45 cm) apart on either side of the upright, as shown, before putting into the soil.

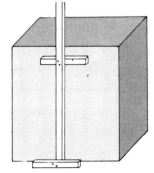

Soft fruits

Raspberries

These grow on canes, about 6 canes to a plant, and are usually trained against or between wires. The early varieties fruit in July and with careful planning with mid to late and autumn-fruiting varieties you can pick raspberries for many months.

Gooseberries

Gooseberries, first of the soft fruits to ripen, can be grown as bushes or cordons. They bear large oval-shaped berries with a semi-transparent, slightly hairy skin and may be green, yellow or red in colour when ripe. The berries can be picked from June onwards.

Blackcurrants

Blackcurrants grow as bushes, but unlike red currants and gooseberries, whose branches grow from the main stem, their branches originate below the soil. The best fruit grows on wood of the previous season.

Red and white currants

Red and white currants differ from blackcurrants. They can be grown as bushes, cordons or half-standards, and the fruit grows on wood up to 10 years old. They flower before blackcurrants and for a longer period and their branches grow out from the main stem.

Requirements	Cultivation	Harvesting
They like well-composted soil, supplemented by spring mulching, on a site sheltered from cold winds. Plant the canes about 2 ft (60 cm) apart, in rows 5–6 ft (1.5–1.8 m) apart. Plant firmly and cut back canes to about 9 in (22 cm).	Mulch in late spring to keep soil moist; dress with sulphate of potash in late winter or early spring. Completely remove all canes that have fruited and reduce new growth to 6 strong canes.	When picking berries leave the core on the stem. The fruit deteriorates rapidly so should be eaten soon after picking. Those not eaten as a dessert can be made into jam. Raspberries can be frozen.
The plants need a good but not too rich soil and should not be exposed to intense sunlight. Grown as cordons plant 18 in (45 cm) apart, and as bushes 4–5 ft (1.2–1.5 m) apart. Bushes are usually two to three years old when bought.	To avoid disturbing roots just below the surface, weed by hand rather than hoe. Mulch well in spring. In February prune by cutting back cordons by about 6 in (15 cm) and laterals to 3 buds. Bushes should be pruned similarly, keeping the centre of the bush open to air and sun.	Unripe berries may be picked for cooking, but only ripe ones for dessert. Gooseberries can be bottled or frozen, made into jam, cooked in pies or eaten as a dessert.
Best grown in medium loam with plenty of humus. One- or two-year-old bushes should be planted 4 ft (1.2 m) apart in rows 6–7 ft (1.8–2.1 m) apart. Prune back the canes to just above soil level.	Weed by hand and mulch during growth. Feed with nitrogen fertiliser in early spring. Protect from wind at flowering time. Prune after harvesting by cutting out those shoots that have fruited. Net, or stretch thread against birds.	Currants picked for keeping or jam-making should be dry and firm. Otherwise they should be black, juicy and becoming soft. Blackcurrants can be bottled or frozen. They are particularly rich in Vitamin C.
They will grow in almost any soil, but well-composted or manured soil helps. Protect from high winds, which may snap branches. Plant cordons about 2 ft (60 cm) apart and bushes 4–5 ft (1.2–1.5 m) apart. Prune leaders and laterals (see pages 122–123) after planting.	Give a top-dressing of a potash fertiliser in early spring when laterals should be pruned to 1–2 in (2–5 cm) and leaders to about 9 in (22 cm). Keep centre of bushes open by cutting out unwanted growth. Remove any suckers.	To avoid damaging the berries they should be picked as sprays with the stalk attached; care should be taken not to damage the spurs, which will bear next year's crop. The fruit is used to make jam and jelly, and can be frozen.

Strawberry

A small, low-growing plant with white flowers and large, fleshy, sweet berries that ripen in the sun and become red. They are usually grown in special beds but can be grown in containers including barrels with holes through which the berries protrude.

Blackberry and loganberry

Blackberries, and to a lesser extent loganberries, make more vigorous growth than raspberries and need stronger support. The taste of the loganberry is not unlike that of the raspberry but it is less sweet and the berry is larger and darker in colour. Cultivated blackberries are larger and more luscious than the wild variety.

Fruit trees

Pruning

Pruning is done partly to allow light and air to get to the centre of the bush or tree and to produce a well-shaped tree, but mainly to encourage vigorous growth and fruiting. Pruning of established fruit trees such as apples or pears in the winter encourages wood growth; that in the summer encourages fruit buds. Winter pruning is done after the leaves have fallen; summer pruning is done in July, beginning with early varieties.

Prune lightly when growth is strong, more severely when growth is weak. Generally, with apples and pears, in summer pruning cut a selection of laterals leaving 5 or 6 leaves from the base. Do not touch leaders. In winter pruning, cut a selection of laterals leaving 4 or 5 buds, and cut down leaders by about one third to one half. Try to leave outgrowing buds.

Some varieties of apples and pears produce their fruit at the tip of the laterals (e.g. Bramley Seedling and Worcester Pearmain) and in these

Planting strawberries
Keep the growing point well above soil level by planting as for fruit trees: i.e. make a small mound in the centre of the hole, spreading the roots downwards before filling in.

Well-drained soil, exposed to the sun, well manured and with slight lime content is best. Late varieties need to be kept well watered. Plant 18 in (45 cm) apart in rows 2–2½ ft (60–75 cm) apart.

When berries begin to turn pink, beds should be netted to protect the fruit from birds. Straw should be placed under the fruit to protect from mud splashes and slugs. Plants should be renewed after the fourth season. Runners should be pinched out unless new plants are needed.

Pick the fruit with the stalk on as it ripens. The fruit deteriorates rapidly, so it should be used as soon as possible. Strawberries can be eaten as a dessert, made into jam, or frozen.

Like raspberries, both flourish in moist soil and respond to generous feeding. Their roots spread widely, as do the canes, and they should be planted (one- or two-year-old plants) between 10 and 12 ft (3–3.6 m) apart and supported by wires or fences.

They are usually trained in the shape of a fan with fruiting canes spread out to right and left and the new canes up the centre. When the fruited canes are cut out after harvesting, the others are trained to take their place; the process is repeated every year.

When picking, the core of the berry should be picked too. Both fruits can be eaten as dessert, or made into jam or jelly. Both can be stored bottled or frozen.

cases only those laterals more than 7 or 8 in (17–20 cm) long should be pruned. The others should be left to fruit that season. Always use a sharp pruning knife and cut cleanly at an angle of 45° just above a wood bud. Pruning of cordons and espaliers is dealt with on pages 118–119. Remember always to paint over large pruning cuts with horticultural bitumen to prevent disease.

Pruning of soft fruit depends on the variety of fruit. Raspberries are cut back to about 5 ft (1.5 m) in early spring and all canes that have fruited are removed, as well as the weaker unfruited canes after harvesting. Gooseberries are cut back by about 6 in (15 cm) and laterals to 3 buds in February. With blackcurrants the shoots that have borne fruit are cut out after harvesting. With red and white currants leaders are cut back to about 9 in (22 cm) and laterals to 1–2 in (2–5 cm) in early spring.

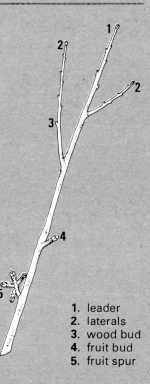

1. leader
2. laterals
3. wood bud
4. fruit bud
5. fruit spur

Requirements

Peach

A hothouse, or even a garden wall, is not necessary for growing peaches. They are, in fact, rather hardy growers and they do well outdoors in a sheltered position if the soil is right. If not to be grown against a wall, they are usually planted as bush trees.

Choose an open and sunny site but one that is not windswept. Soil should be moist but properly drained and have sufficient lime and organic matter. Plant one- or two-year-old bushes about 18 ft (5.5 m) apart. Cut back the main leaders by about 1 ft (30 cm) after planting.

Plum

Plums cover a wide range, including the large plums that we all know, damsons, mirabelles and bullaces, and greengages. They are best grown as bush trees or half-standards but if you are lucky enough to have a wall they can be grown as fans.

Plums do not like acid soil so lime deficiency should be rectified. When planting bush or half-standard trees dig a hole 3 ft (90 cm) in diameter and put some well-rotted compost in it. After planting, firm soil down well. Plant bushes 12 ft (3.7 m) apart, half-standards 15 ft (4.6 m) apart.

Pear

The cultivation of pear trees is similar to that of apples. The easiest type to grow are the bush trees but pears lend themselves readily to training. Varieties that fruit on tips of laterals (see pages 122–123), such as Jargonelle and Josephine de Malines can not be trained.

Pears will grow in almost any soil except wet clay but they prefer a warm soil that is fairly rich and well drained. Dig in compost before planting. When planting be sure that the graft point on the stem is not covered by soil. Distances between trees should be much the same as with apples.

Apple

Varieties of apple are many, ranging through early, mid-season and late dessert varieties to late cookers such as Bramley's Seedling. There are almost as many types of tree: bush (perhaps the most suitable for small gardens or allotments), dwarf pyramids, cordons and espaliers, half-standards and standards.

Apple trees are not choosy about soil but they like good drainage. Autumn is best for planting, and two- or three-year-old trees are preferable. Stake standards or half-standards. Plant bush trees from 8–12 ft (2.4–3.6 m) apart, dwarf pyramids about the same, and standards or half-standards up to 25 ft (7.6 m).

Mulch generously with compost in the spring. After buds have opened thin out excessive shoots; remove laterals that have fruited (the fruit comes on two-year-old wood); cut off any dead tips on remaining shoots. Thin out fruit when nut-size, to about 9 in (22 cm) apart.

Peaches are best picked when fully ripe, i.e. when they come away from their stalk easily. Handle gently, because the fruit bruises easily. Peaches can be bottled or frozen.

For the first few years mulch in the spring. Little pruning is required beyond removing dead wood and overcrowding in late spring or late autumn. Plums fruit on old wood so gradually eliminate the older wood to have as much new wood as possible. Remove any suckers that grow,

Pick cooking plums as soon as they begin to colour. Dessert plums will not keep for more than a few days. They should be handled carefully, and watch out for wasps that have burrowed into the fruit. Plums can be bottled or made into jam.

Apply mulch in spring and a dressing of sulphate of ammonia in February or March. In early winter prune leaders by one third. Cut laterals to 4 or 5 buds. In July, cut back laterals to 5 or 6 leaves from the base. With tip-bearing varieties prune only laterals more than 6–8 in (15–20 cm) long.

When pears are picked for keeping is highly important; they will not store well if gathered too soon or too late. If the fruit separates from the spur readily when lifted to a horizontal position it is ready. Store as for apples, but wrapping is not necessary. Store away from strong smells. Pears in store need constant watching as they remain in good condition for only a short time when ripened. Pears can also be preserved in jars.

Apples require little cultivation as such. If the soil is light, mulch in the summer and spread wood ash in December. Winter and summer pruning (see pages 122–123) is time-consuming. Thin out heavy crops, but don't forget the natural drop in June.

If, when raised and twisted slightly, the fruit with the stalk comes away in your hand, it is ready to be harvested. Dessert apples need to be ripe when picked or they will not gain their full flavour. Pick the fruit gently to avoid bruising. Many apples store well in a cool, dark place in trays allowing the air to circulate. They can be wrapped in oiled paper or kept in large ventilated plastic bags. Never store diseased or damaged apples.

Methods of storing

There are many different ways of storing the vegetables and fruit you have grown. They are best eaten fresh, of course, but part of the fun and skill of growing them is to spread their use out over the winter months. In any case some — such as potatoes — crop so heavily that a very large family indeed would be needed to use them all up as they mature. So potatoes are stored dry in boxes, bags or clamps; but other crops, such as beans and peas, can only be kept by bottling or freezing. The table below shows the different ways in which fruit and vegetables can be stored and in the following pages you can learn how to bottle, pickle or freeze and how to make preserves.

	Apple	Beans (Broad, French, Runner)	Beetroots	Blackberries	Blackcurrants	Broccoli spears	Brussel sprouts	Carrots	Cauliflower (young)	Cabbage (red)	Garlic	Gooseberries	Leeks
Clamp			▲					▲					
Dry Storage	◇		◇					◇			◇		
Bottled or Preserved	●			●	●							●	
Pickled			●						●	●			
Dried	●	●											
Salted		●											
Jams or Jellies	●			●	●							●	
Frozen		●	●	●	●	●	●	●	●			●	●
In the ground													●

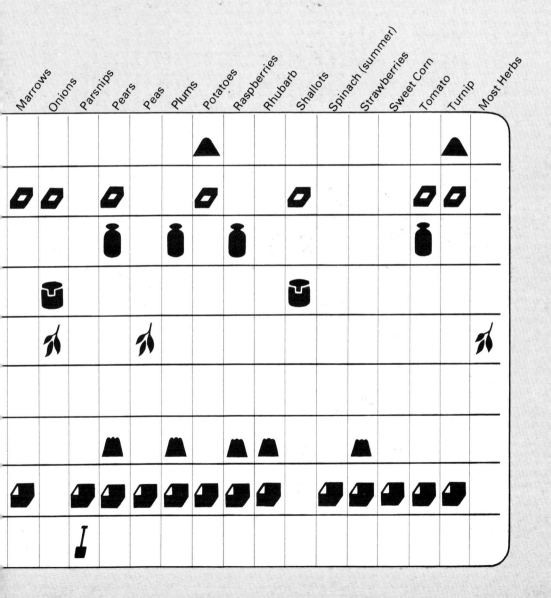

Storing outdoors and in

Most of the root vegetables opposite pose problems of bulk storage; green vegetables can also be stored, mainly by freezing. If you haven't a freezer, you can preserve beans in the old-fashioned way by salting them down in a crock. Lettuce, cucumber, marrows and tomatoes are unsuitable for freezing because of their high water content. Most usual and most convenient for freezing are peas, beans, brussels sprouts, young cauliflowers, baby carrots and beetroots, and sweet corn.

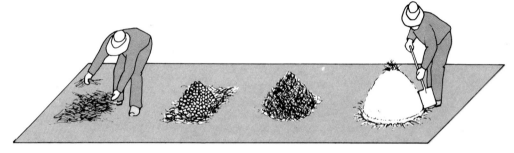

How to clamp

For storing root crops in bulk outdoors you need to make a clamp. Choose a well-protected part of the garden and lay down some straw or clinker. Make a base of your crop on this and build up into pyramid form. Cover the pyramid with a layer of straw 4–6 in (10–15 cm) thick and then cover the whole thing with soil of the same thickness dug out from around the clamp. Make a hole in the top of the clamp and pull out a little of the straw to provide ventilation.

Freezing vegetables

Yes	No
beans	tomatoes
shelled peas	lettuce
baby carrots	cucumbers
baby beetroots	marrows
young cauliflower	onions
brussels sprouts	most mature root crops
summer spinach	
sweet corn	

Storing vegetables indoors

Beetroot
can be stored in boxes in peat or slightly damp soil. Make a base of the peat or sand, then lay the beetroot neatly on it, first twisting (not cutting) off the leaves about 2 in (5 cm) above the root. Repeat process till box is full. Keep in dry cool place, free from frost.

Carrots
as above.

Leeks
can remain in the ground till required.

Marrows
will keep for some time if suspended in netting allowing air to circulate freely.

Onions
can be strung (see page 92) or stored in wooden trays or boxes with ventilated bottoms.

Parsnips
can be left in the ground. If this is not possible, leave them in a heap in a corner of the allotment.

Potatoes
if not being stored in bulk outdoors (see page 128) can be stored in boxes or trays, sacks or plastic bags. It is essential that air should be let in and light kept out. Line and top boxes with straw or newspaper.

Shallots
are best stored in boxes like onions, first removing the leaves and flaky outside skins.

Tomatoes
can be stored in trays or drawers until ripe or whole trusses of green tomatoes can be hung indoors until ready.

Turnips
are stored by the same methods as potatoes, carrots and beetroot.

No ice please
A garage, cellar, shed or unheated room does well for storage but it is essential it should be frostproof.

On the shelf – bottling

The principle of bottling both vegetables and fruit is to preserve them in liquids in jars from which the air has been driven by heating. If the cap is screwed on tightly while the hot liquid is over the brim of the jar a vacuum will be created when the liquid contracts on cooling in the now airtight container.

There are three methods of heating for bottling: with a pressure cooker (1), in heated water in a large pan (2) or in the oven (3). Vegetables should be bottled only with a pressure cooker: other methods are unsafe. Fruits may be bottled by all three methods. The two water methods require a large pan capable of holding several jars, with a false bottom to keep the jars from the main source of heat. The jars may be put in to cold water, which is then brought to the boil, or into already boiling water (190°F/88°C). The latter is the quicker and more usual method. Vegetables or fruit should be packed tightly into clean hot jars, which are then filled with usually salted water in the case of vegetables and syrup or water in the case of fruit. With the cold water method the brine or syrup should be cold; with the hot water method, hot. (For timing see opposite.) With the oven method the jars, filled with soft fruit and syrup or water, are put, loosely covered, into the oven at 300°F (150°C) and kept there for the appropriate period.

To salt down beans use a large crock. Slice runner beans; use only tender young French beans – no need to slice. Put a layer of salt in the bottom of a large crock, then a layer of beans, then salt and so on, pressing down firmly. Use about 1 lb (0.45 kg) of salt to 3 lb (1.4 kg) of beans. When crock is full, cover and keep in a cool place. When used, beans are washed and soaked in water for 2 hours to remove salt.

The method you use for bottling will depend partly on what tools you already have. A pressure cooker (1) or a very large pan (2) may already be in your kitchen; but an oven (3) you will surely have, and this can be used for bottling fruits, though not vegetables. But if you intend to do a lot of bottling, (1) or (2) will soon save you as much as they cost.

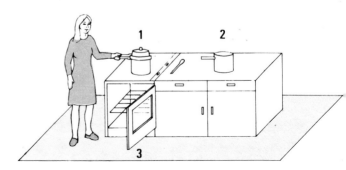

Vegetable	Pressure cooker time (for 1 pt [0.5 l] jars at 10 lb [4.5 kg])	Preparation (Brine = ¾ teaspoon salt per 1 pt [0.5 l] liquid)
Asparagus	25 min	Break off tough part of stem, add brine.
Beans (French and runner)	20 min	Slice or leave whole, scald 3 min, add brine.
Beetroot (small)	25 min	Cook whole 15 min. Peel, use water with 1 teaspoon vinegar, not brine.
Broccoli	30 min	Soak in salt water, scald 3 min, add brine.
Carrots (small)	20 min	Wash, scald 3 min, add brine.
Cauliflower	30 min	As for broccoli.
Shelled peas	40 min	Scald 3 min, add brine.

Soft Fruits	Hot water method	Pressure Cooker at 5 lb (2.2 kg)	Oven Method at 300°F (150°C)	
			up to 4 lb (1.8 kg)	5–10 lb (2.2–4.5 kg)
Raspberries Loganberries Blackberries	190°F (88°C), 2 min	1 min	30–40 min	45–60 min
Strawberries	as above	not applicable	as above	as above
Gooseberries (cooking)	as above	1 min	as above	as above
(dessert)	190°F (88°C), 10 min	1 min	40–50 min	55–70 min
Currants	as above	1 min	as above	as above
Rhubarb (cooking)	190°F (88°C), 2 min	1 min	30–40 min	45–60 min
(dessert)	190°F (88°C), 10 min	1 min	40–50 min	55–70 min
Tomatoes (whole)	190°F (88°C), 40 min	5 min	60–70 min	75–90 min

Preparation Pick off stalks etc, reject damaged fruit. Hull strawberries and rinse in cold water. Top and tail gooseberries. Tomatoes may be peeled or skin left on.

Syrup If bottling in syrup use ½ lb (226 g) of sugar to 1 pt water. Bring to the boil, stirring to dissolve the sugar, and boil for 1 minute.

Skin tight
If you are bottling gooseberries in syrup prick the skins or the berries may shrivel.

On the shelf - jams

By no means the least agreeable way of preserving the fruits of your allotment or garden is to make them into jam or jelly. Jams don't have to be made only from fruit, however; the humble vegetable marrow, with an appropriate mixture of root ginger, makes excellent jam, as does rhubarb.

Basically jam-making is a very simple operation. Boil your fruit with sugar until it sets and there you are. But, as with most simple things, there are tricks that help to produce a better result. What makes the jam set is something in the fruit called pectin, so the first thing you do, having prepared the fruit, is boil and allow it to cool, because this brings out the pectin. Then test the fruit to see how much pectin there really is (see below) because this determines the ratio of sugar to fruit that you will use.

Add the appropriate amount of sugar to the fruit in the pan – the sugar will dissolve more easily if warmed in a slow oven beforehand –

Jam can certainly be made in small quantities in a small pan but for jam-making to be worthwhile a large preserving pan is essential, and a long-handled wooden spoon. The bottom of the pan should be wiped with a piece of buttered paper to prevent burning.

A time-tested way of straining, if you do not have a jelly bag, is to tie a cloth to the four legs of an upturned stool, placing the receiving bowl on the upturned seat.

To test for pectin pour 1 teaspoonful of juice into a warm glass. When cool pour in 3 teaspoonsful of methylated spirit, shake gently and allow to stand for a few minutes. If a solid, fair-size clot of pectin forms, the supply is adequate and you use 1¼ lb (0.6 kg) of sugar to each pound of fruit. If the globule is broken into two or three parts use 1 lb (454 g) of sugar to the same of fruit. If it is in many parts the pectin is low and you should use ¾ lb (339 g) of sugar to each pound of fruit.

Strawberry
Use small strawberries. Hull them, and put them in the pan alternating with layers of sugar. Do not add any water. Use same weight of sugar as strawberries. Bring to boil *very* slowly, stirring occasionally, until sugar is dissolved. Additional pectin can be added in the form of redcurrant or gooseberry juice. When sugar is dissolved, bring to boil quickly and remove from heat. When skin forms on top, jam is ready.

and bring to the boil. The jam is done when the liquid sets when cooled on a saucer. The scum is skimmed off and the jam poured into jars, which can be sealed with waxed paper and cellulose covers tied down with string or a rubber band.

Jellies

A jelly is really jam without the fruit in it: that is, the juice is extracted and then cooked with sugar until it sets. Because you will strain off the juice, the preparation of the fruit is less than that needed for jam. Simply wash it and cut hard fruits such as apples into small pieces: no need to peel or core, or to remove stems etc from soft fruits. Put in the pan barely covering with water and simmer until the fruit is soft, then strain through a jelly bag into a large bowl. Test for pectin as with jam and adjust sugar weight accordingly. Dissolve sugar in the juice in a pan and boil rapidly until setting point is reached, as with jam. Pour into jars.

> **Don't squeeze**
> *When straining juice don't squeeze the bag or the jelly will go cloudy.*

Below are recipes for four favourite jams. The sugar used can be granulated, cube or preserving.

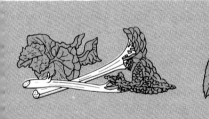

Rhubarb
Use the same amount of sugar as rhubarb. Remove outer stringy part and cut sticks into small sections, put a layer in a bowl, cover with sugar and repeat. Leave overnight. Transfer to pan and add the rind and juice of a lemon. Suspend 2 oz (57 g) bruised root ginger in a muslin bag in the pan and bring to the boil very slowly, stirring occasionally until setting point is reached.

Greengage or Plum
Allow ¾ lb (339 g) of sugar to 1 lb (454 g) of fruit. Remove stems and stones of fruit, cracking a few of the latter and keeping kernels. Boil fruit and kernels in ½ in (1 cm) of water gently for 15 minutes. Then add sugar gradually, continuing boiling until setting point is reached.

Blackberry and Apple
Stew 4 lb (1.4 kg) blackberries (poor in pectin) in ¼ pt (0.2 l) of water until tender, remove seeds by passing through a sieve. Peel 1½ lb (679 g) apples (rich in pectin), remove cores and slice. Boil until tender in ¼ pt (0.2 l) water. Add blackberries and boil until thick. Weigh the result, return to pan with equal weight of sugar and boil rapidly until setting point.

On the shelf – pickles and chutneys

Another time-honoured way of storing vegetables is by pickling them in spiced vinegar. An old recipe for this using the ingredients below is:

¼ oz (7 g) cinnamon bark	some peppercorns
¼ oz (7 g) cloves	½ oz (14 g) root ginger
¼ oz (7 g) mace	2 bay leaves
¼ oz (7 g) allspice	1 qt (1.1 l) vinegar

Use spices whole – not ground – and tie them in a muslin bag. Put it in a pan, add the vinegar and 1 tablespoonful of salt, cover the pan and allow to stand for a week. Then boil for 5 minutes, allow to stand for 2 hours, remove spice bag and strain vinegar into jars ready for use. Never prepare the vinegar in a copper, brass or iron pan; all kinds of vinegar can be used. Be sure the jars can be properly closed and that no metal comes in contact with the spiced vinegar.

It's in the bag
When pickling or making chutney, as with using a bouquet garni *in stew, attach the muslin bag to the handle of the pan so that you can extract it without difficulty.*

Beetroot
Boil until tender but do not allow the skins to be damaged or the root will lose colour. Peel and cut when cool into slices or dice. Pack into jar and cover with spiced vinegar. If they are to be stored for a considerable time use boiling vinegar, otherwise cold.

Cabbage
The cabbage should be firm and a good colour. Remove outer leaves, cut in quarters, remove centre stalk and shred remainder on a large dish. Sprinkle well with salt and leave for 24 hours. Drain off the brine that will have formed, put into pickling jar and cover with cold spiced vinegar. Don't keep for too long or it may lose its crispness.

Onions
Use small onions, which should be ripe and dry. Soak in brine (¼ lb (113 g) salt to 1 qt (1.1 l water) for 12 hours. Then peel and leave them covered in new brine for 24 hours. Wash well in cold water, drain thoroughly and pack in jars, covering with cold spiced vinegar. Keep for 3 months before using.

A combination of any of the fruits and vegetables shown above can go into a chutney, which is particularly useful as a way of storing over-ripe material or green tomatoes. In general the fruit or vegetables are finely chopped, vinegar, sugar, herbs and spices are added to taste and the whole is cooked very slowly so that the liquid evaporates. Use dark sugar if you want a dark chutney. Chutneys are very much a matter of personal taste but here is one way of making a tomato chutney using the ingredients shown on the left:

4 lb (1.8 kg) green tomatoes
½ lb (227 g) granulated sugar
juice of 2 lemons
4 lb (1.8 kg) apples
1 lb (454 g) sultanas
1 oz (28 g) root ginger
½ oz (14 g) red chillies
1 lb (454 g) shallots
3 oz (84 g) salt
3 pt (1.7 l) vinegar

Tie the ginger and chillies in a muslin bag and simmer, stirring frequently for 4 hours until the chutney is like a thick jam. Remove muslin bag and bottle while still hot in clean hot jars. Seal well.

Gherkins
Soak the small ridge cucumbers in brine (see onions) for 3 days. Strain and pack into bottles, then fill with boiling spiced vinegar. Add 1 tablespoonful of dill seed and a spring of dill to each jar. Strain and reboil the vinegar and pour back over gherkins.

Walnuts
You are not likely to have a walnut tree in your allotment, but you may have one in your garden. Use young green walnuts. Prick them well with a steel fork and cover with strong brine for a week, stirring 2 or 3 times daily. Repeat in fresh brine for a week, drain and spread them out on dishes in the sun until they are black. Pack in jars and cover with cold spiced vinegar made with 1 oz (28 g) peppercorns, 1 oz (28 g) allspice and 1 teaspoonful of salt to each quart of vinegar, boiled for 15 minutes.

Eggs
And if you keep hens, why not pickle the spare eggs? Hard-boil and shell them, pack in jars and cover with spiced vinegar — 1 pt (0.5 l) will do for 6 eggs.

Storing by degrees

The sooner your vegetables get into the freezer after gathering, the better. But they need to be cleaned, trimmed and blanched before going into the freezer. Blanching is a process of quick boiling to kill bacteria. The vegetables are plunged into boiling water, left there for a few minutes, then chilled in ice water and drained off.

Blanching times from moment of immersion in boiling water		
	1 min	Shelled peas
	2 min	French and runner beans, spinach, kale
	2½ min	Beetroot (small)
	3 min	Broad beans, broccoli, small carrots, cauliflower
	3½ min	Asparagus
	4 min	Brussels sprouts, celery, sweet corn off the cob.
	6 min plus	Sweet corn on the cob.

How to Prepare

Asparagus	Break off tough ends, remove scales.
Broad beans	Shell before blanching.
French and runner beans	Remove stem end, cut into 2–3 in (5–7 cm) pieces or lengthwise.
Beetroots	Use only baby beets. Blanch, chill then peel. Can be left whole or sliced.
Broccoli	Soak in salt water for 30 min after removing coarse stem and peeling stalks. Split lengthwise.
Brussels sprouts	Stand in salt water for 30 min. Remove loose outer leaves – blanch, chill and drain.
Carrots	Use only baby carrots, remove tops, Wash and peel, blanch, chill and drain.
Cauliflower	Stand in salt water for 30 min. Break into florets. Blanch in salt water, chill and drain.
Celery	Wash and cut in small pieces. Blanch, chill and drain.
Peas	Shell, blanch, chill and drain.
Sweet corn	Remove husks and silks. Blanch, chill and drain. Cut kernels from cob or freeze cobs whole.

There are two ways of freezing soft fruits: in syrup or in sugar. The syrup may be *heavy* (4 cups of water to 6–7 cups of sugar), *medium* (4 cups water to 4–6 cups sugar), or *thin* (4 cups water to 2–3 cups sugar). When freezing in sugar add the sugar to the fruit, and stir very lightly so as not to damage the fruit. Let stand for 20 min before freezing.

Packing
Use preferably square airtight containers. Leave a small space at the top. Label and date container. Place container against freezer walls but leaving space for air to circulate. When using frozen vegetables cook while frozen, i.e. don't thaw them out. *Never* re-freeze.

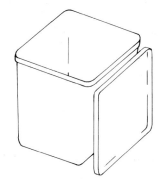

Frost without freezing.
An attractive Christmas table decoration can be made by frosting fruit. Choose brightly coloured fruit – red apples, yellow pears, grapes etc. Dip the fruit first into beaten egg, then into caster sugar. The fruit seems to have been dusted by frost.

How to Prepare

Raspberries
Blackberries
Gooseberries
Sort, remove any stems etc, wash in ice water and drain well. Pack dry as they are *or* cover with medium syrup *or* pack in sugar, 1 lb (0.45 kg) sugar to 5–6 lb (2.3–2.7 kg) fruit.

Strawberries
Carefully choose the best berries, sort and hull. Wash in ice water and drain. Pack whole in medium syrup *or* sliced in sugar, 1 lb (0.45 kg) sugar to 5–6 lb (2.3–2.7 kg) fruit. Berries can be frozen whole without sugar: wash in ice water, drain thoroughly. Separate fruit on shallow dish and freeze. When frozen, pack in container.

Rhubarb
Wash stems, trim, cut into 2–3 in (5–7 cm) pieces, drain well. Pack in medium syrup *or* in sugar, *or* blanch, chill, drain and freeze.

From garden to allotment

With the prices of vegetables rocketing it is not surprising that many gardeners are transforming flower gardens into vegetable plots. It is not difficult and often a reasonable compromise can be reached by converting only a part. Many vegetables look attractive, and in any case it is easy to screen off the end of the garden with a row of sweet peas or runner beans and have a small vegetable plot behind it. Do you really need all that lawn? Many herbs look quite decorative in the flower beds and parsley plants spaced between roses make a most attractive contrast.

Certainly you don't need much space to grow catch crops such as lettuces and radishes between two rows of peas or slow-growing Brussels sprouts. It's true that the latter have to be spaced well apart but you can expect as much as 2 lb (0.9 kg) of sprouts from each plant. Carrots and leeks don't take up much room and you can get 10 or 12 shallots for every one you plant. If it is to be really worthwhile growing potatoes, you may have to sacrifice a biggish slice of lawn, but do look at the flowerbeds and consider whether some of them might not be more usefully employed.

Sun-bathed fences or walls are splendid for peas, tomatoes, runner beans or fruit of some sort. One advantage of converting established gardens into allotments is that the soil in the beds has already been reduced to a fine tilth and perhaps even manured or composted. As a rough guide you can estimate that if you had a part of your garden to spare 33 ft (10 m) by 12 ft (3.6 m) you could grow enough salads, beetroot, carrots, peas and runner beans to feed a family of four in the summer and enough cabbage, broccoli, brussels sprouts and leeks for the winter. The plan below shows how you could create such a vegetable patch at the end of a garden, say, 40 ft (12.2 m) by 30 ft (9.2 m).

On the record

With the ending of the year, your shelves groaning with produce preserved in one form or another, the great clamps of potatoes and root crops standing in the allotment as a background to the rows of sturdy brussels sprouts and other winter greens, and above all with the reduction in the number of hours it is possible to work outdoors, comes that 'something attempted, something done, has earned a night's repose' feeling. But before you take full advantage of it do a little paper work. Don't forget that it's a time not only for looking back but also for looking forward.

To begin with you should keep some sort of record. You will want to remember which crops did particularly well, and where, as a guide to next year's growing. You'll want to record any unusual features of particular patches of soil — exceptional wetness etc. Don't rely too much on your memory, for it has a good deal to cope with and the things most easily forgotten are your own mistakes. You'll certainly want to remember which seed varieties served you well and any that served you badly; what insecticides you used and when; which fertilizers and manures you dug in and when; where you put on top-dressings and where base, and particularly which parts of the allotment you limed and when.

All change
Make a plan of your allotment and mark in where your crops went this year so that you can rotate them correctly next year (see pages 54–55).

It's a date
Make a note on next year's calendar of when you should feed your garden in relation to the food you gave it last year. Make a note when to order seeds, fertilisers and (if possible) manure.

Rising prizes
Keep a graph in the kitchen showing the trend of vegetable prices in the shops: when they touch the top etc. Within reason and season you can seek to match this with a growing graph.

Back up
NB To be up to date this book, too, is 'index-linked.' The index is on the next three pages.

Spring is the allotment grower's busiest time, and help is always welcome from young enthusiasts.

Index

A
Acid soils, 27, 85
Allotment holders, association of, 12
Allotments Acts, 11
Allotments, area of, 10–11
Animals, keeping of, 12
Annuals, 16; weeds, 22
Ants, 111
Applemint, 107
Apples, 16, 122–123, 124–125, 126–127; Blackberry and, 133
Artichokes: Chinese, 83; Globe, 98; Jerusalem, 48, 82
Asparagus, 24, 25, 48–49, 97, 131, 136
Asparagus pea, 88
Aubergines, 105

B
Bacteria, 27
Bags, 7
Base-dressing, 16, 42, 43, 140
Basil, 108
Bay, 107
Beans, 54–55, 84–86, 126–127, 128; broad, 39, 48–49, 53, 60, 61, 84–85, 113, 136; French, 39, 49–50, 53, 59, 60, 61, 84–85, 130, 131, 136; runner, 49, 53, 59, 60, 61, 84–86, 131, 136
Bedding-out plants, 7
Beds, 24
Bees, 110
Beetroot, 23, 49, 53, 59, 60, 61, 76, 113, 126–127, 128, 129, 131, 134, 136
Biennials, 16
Bindweed, 21, 23
Birds, 32, 110
Blackberries, 122–123, 126–127, 131, 137; and apple, 133

Blackcurrants, 120–121, 123, 131
Blackfly, 85, 113
Black nightshade, 22
Blanching: (boiling) 16, 136; (whitening) 16, 90, 94–95; self-, 95
Bolting, 16
Bone meal, 43
Bonfires, 20, 22, 24, 25, 112
Boot scraper, 24, 25
Borage, 106
Bordeaux mixture, 80
Borders, 25
Bottling, 126–127, 130–131
Bouquet garni, 107, 109, 134
Brassicas, 16, 54–55, 57, 58–59, 64–69, 82, 113
Broccoli, 49–50, 53, 59, 60, 61, 67, 126–127, 131, 136
Brussels sprouts, 10, 46–47, 48–49, 51, 53, 59, 60, 61, 66, 126–127, 128, 136
Buckets, 7

C
Cabbage caterpillar, 53, 113
Cabbage gall weevil, 65
Cabbage lettuce, 70, 71
Cabbage root fly, 65
Cabbages, 39, 48–51, 53, 59, 60, 61, 64–65, 134; Chinese, 49–50, 65; red, 48, 50, 64, 126–127
Calcium, 27, 42: deficiency, 26
Calendar of gardening, 48–51
Cardoon, 99
Carrots, 10, 39, 48–50, 53, 58–59, 60, 61, 74–75, 113, 126–127, 128, 129, 131, 136
Catch crops, 16, 25
Cats, 32
Cauliflower, 39, 48–49, 53, 59, 60, 61, 68, 126–127, 128, 131, 136
Cauliflower ear, 142
Celeriac, 49, 82
Celery, 49, 51, 53, 61, 94–95, 113, 136; turnip-rooted, 82
Celtuce, 72
Chafer grubs, 113
Chalky soil, 26–27
Charlock, 22
Chervil, 83, 106, 109
Chickweed, 22
Chicory, 49, 98
Chitting, 81
Chives, 106, 109
Chutney, 134, 135
Clamps, 75, 81, 126–127, 128

Clay soil, 26–27
Cloches, 16, 36, 38–39; care of, 39
Club root, 64
Colorado beetle, 81
Compost, 7, 16, 22, 24, 27, 34, 42, 43, 44–45, 49, 56: bins, 44
Cordoned fruit trees, 25, 117
Corn on the cob, *see* Sweet corn
Corn salad, 72
Cos lettuce, 70, 71
Couch grass, 23, 33, 35
Courgettes, 49, 105
Cress, mustard and, 73
Cross-pollinating fruit trees, 116
Cucumbers, 49, 61, 104, 128; outdoor, 60
Currants, *see* Blackcurrants, etc.
Cutworms, 65, 111, 113

D
Damages, 32, 33
Dandelions, 23
Deficiencies, signs of, 26
Dibber, 29, 52, 57
Digging, 19, 34–35
Dill, 108, 109
Discount facilities, 12
Diseases, 17, 55, 112–113
Distances between plants, 52–53
Docks, 21, 23, 33
Dogs, 32
Double-digging, 34–35, 110
Drainage, 20, 21, 27, 35, 45, 110
Draw hoe, 28
Dressing, *see* Top-dressing, Base-dressing
Drills, 52–53
Dutch hoe, 28

E
Earthing up, 16
Earthworms, 27, 111
Edgecutter, 29
Eggs, pickling, 135
Enclosure, 11
Endive, 49–50, 53, 73
Escarole, 73
Espaliered fruit trees, 25, 117

F
Fanned fruit trees, 25
Fences, 20, 24, 25; repair of, 12, 33; wire netting, 32
Fennel, 107, 109; Florence, *see* Finocchio

Fertilisers, 7, 16, 25, 42–43, 140; bags, 7, 30–31; discounts for, 12
Fibrous pots, 31, 57
Fines herbes, 106
Finocchio, 99
Fire insurance, 12
Fish meal, 43
Flea beetle, 65, 78, 79
Florence fennel, *see* Finocchio
Foliar feed, 42, 43
Forcing, 16, 96
Forks, 7, 28
Frames, 25, 36–37
Freezing, 16, 126–127, 128, 136–137
Frosting, 137
Frosts, 38, 40, 81, 129
Fruit cage, 116
Fruit trees, 12, 24, 25, 116–117; pruning, 122–123

G
Gardens, 15; to allotments, 138–139
Garlic, 48, 91, 93, 126–127
Germination, 58–59
Gherkins, pickling, 135
Good King Henry, 73
Gooseberries, 120–121, 123, 126–127, 131, 137
Grass-cuttings, 27, 45
Greenfly, 53, 75, 110, 113
Greengages, 133
Greenhouses, 16, 25, 36, 40
Green manure, 22, 27, 33
Green vegetables, storage of, 128
Ground elder, 21
Growth, 7

H
Half-hardy plants, 16
Hamburg parsley, 83
Hand fork, 29
Hand trowel, 28, 57
Hardening off, 16
Haulms, 16, 80
Heeling in, 16
Hens, keeping of, 12
Herb garden, 25, 106–107
Herbs, 106–109, 138; gathering, 108; storing, 108–109, 126–127
Hoes, 22, 23, 43; *see also* Draw hoe, Dutch hoe
Horseradish, 48, 107
Humidity, 40
Humus, 16, 27, 42, 44, 110

I
Inorganic fertilisers, 42–43
Insecticides, 7, 57, 104, 110, 140
Insect pests, *see* Pests
Inter-cropping, 16, 70

J
Jamjars, 38, 39
Jam-making, 126–127, 132–133
Jellies, 126–127, 132–133
John Innes compost, 37

K
Kale, 49–50, 59, 60, 61, 69, 136
Kohlrabi, 59, 82

L
Labelling, 29, 52, 57, 137
Ladybirds, 110
Landlords, 11, 12
Lateral branches, 117, 122–123
Leatherjackets, 111, 113
Leeks, 48–50, 53, 59, 60, 61, 90, 113, 126–127, 129
Legumes, 54–55, 84–88; *see also* Peas, Beans
Lettuce, 10, 37, 39, 48–50, 51, 53, 58–59, 60, 61, 70–71, 113, 128
Lights, 16
Lime, 27, 42, 140; excessive, 112
Liquid fertilisers, 43
Liquid manure, 43
Loam, 26–27
Local associations of allotment holders, 12
Loganberries, 122–123, 131

M
Maggots, 113
Maiden fruit trees, 16, 117
Mangetout peas, 88
Manure, 7, 19, 27, 34, 36, 42, 43, 49, 140
Marjoram, 108
Marrows, 25, 49, 59, 61, 103, 126–127, 128, 129
Mechanical cultivator, 23
Mice, 32, 85, 87
Mildew, 87
Millipedes, 111, 113
Mint, 107
Mosaic diseases, 70, 103, 104
Mulching, 17, 23
Mustard (and cress), 73

N
National Allotments and Gardens Society Ltd, 12
National Society of Leisure Gardeners Ltd, 12
Nettles, 23
Nitrogen, 26, 42, 43, 54, 87; deficiency, 26
Nuisance to neighbours, 12

O
Onions, 48, 53, 59, 60, 61, 74, 91–93, 113, 126–127, 128, 129; pickling, 134; sets, 93
Organic fertilisers, 42–43
Oyster plant, 83

P
Parsley, 39, 58–59, 108, 109, 138; Hamburg, *see* Hamburg parsley
Parsnips, 48–49, 50, 53, 60, 61, 77, 126–127, 129
Paths, 20, 24, 25, 35; in greenhouse, 41
Peaches, 124–125
Pears, 16, 122–123, 124–125, 126–127
Peas, 10, 39, 48–50, 53, 54–55, 59, 60, 61, 87–88, 113, 126–127, 128, 131, 136; sugar, 88; *see also* Asparagus peas
Peat: bags, 7, 56; pots, *see* Fibrous pots; soil, 26–27
Pectin, 132–133
Perennials, 17; weeds, 21, 22, 23, 33, 34
Perpetual spinach, 72
Pests, 27, 40, 55, 110–111, 113
Petit pois, 88
Phosphate, 42, 43; deficiency, 26
Pickling, 134–135
Pinching out, 17
Plums, 124–125, 133
Poles, 14–15
Potash, 26, 42, 43; deficiency, 26, 112
Potatoes, 10, 17, 27, 48–49, 51, 54–55, 58–59, 80–81, 113, 126–127, 129
Pots, 7, 31, 56, 112
Preserving, 126–137
Prices, 10, 140, 141
Pricking out, 17
Propagator box, 41
Pruning, 17, 28, 118, 122–123
Pruning knife, 29
Pumpkins, 105

R

Rabbits: keeping, 12; as pest, 32

Radishes, 25, 39, 48–50, 51, 58–59, 60, 61, 79, 109

Rake, 28, 43, 57; to mark rows, 52

Rampion, 83

Raspberries, 118–119, 120–121, 126–127, 131, 137

Records, 140–141

Red currants, 120–121, 123

Rents, 12–13

Rhizomes, 17, 23

Rhododendrons, 26

Rhubarb, 25, 96, 126–127, 131, 133, 137; leaves, 112

Ring culture (of tomatoes), 102

Rods, 14–15

Root crops, 42, 74–83; harvesting, 59, 83; storing, 128–129

Rosemary, 107, 109

Rotation of crops, 17, 27, 54–55, 140

Rows, marking of, 52, 57

Rubbish, 7, 111

Runner beans, see Beans, runner

S

Sage, 109

Salsify, 83

Salting, 126–127, 128, 130

Sandy soil, 26–27

Scallions, 91

Schools, gardening in, 13

Scolymus, 83

Scorzonera, 83

Seakale, 39, 48, 97

Seaweed, as manure, 43, 97

Secateurs, 28, 29

Seed bed, 25

Seed boxes (trays), 30, 31, 41, 56, 112

Seedlings, 7, 30, 37, 39, 49, 50, 112; Hardening off, 16, 36; pricking out, 17, 37, 56; thinning out, 17, 39, 52–53, 56

Seeds, 7, 49, 60–61, 140; discounts for, 12; packets, 7, 48, 60; pelleted, 37, 56, 59; prices, 10, 50, 141

Shallots, 48, 53, 59, 91, 93, 126–127, 129, 138

Shears, 28, 29

Shelter, 15

Shepherd's purse, 22

Short-lease allotments, 20

Sickle, 29

Sieve, 29

Site of allotment, 20, 24

Size of allotment, 14–15, 21

Skirret, 83

Slope of allotment, 20

Slugs, 7, 45, 49, 81, 85, 111, 113; pellets, 57

Snails, 45, 111, 113

Sodium chlorate, 23

Soft fruits, 24, 116, 118–123, 130–133

Soil: exhaustion, 17; testing, 26; types, 14, 20, 26–27

Sorrel, 72

Sowing: dates, 7, 39; techniques, 52–53, 56–57

Spades, 7, 24, 28, 31

Speedwell, 22

Spinach, 39, 48–50, 53, 59, 60, 61, 72, 126–127, 128, 136

Spinach beet, 72

Spit (definition) 34

Spring onions, 91

Sprouts, see Brussels sprouts

Stopping, 17

Storage, 7, 126–137

Strawberries, 24, 25, 118–119, 122–123, 126–127, 131, 132, 137

Subsoil, 34

Successional sowing, 17

Suckers, 17

Swat (sickle), 29

Sweet corn, 49, 61, 89, 126–127, 128, 136

Sweet (green) peppers, 49, 105

Swiss chard, 73

Syringes, 7

Syrup, 131, 137

T

Tarragon, 106

Tenancy agreements, 12

Thieves, 30, 31, 33

Thinning out, 17

Thistles, 21, 23, 33

Thongs, 97

Thrips, 83, 113

Thyme, 109

Tilth, 17, 23, 28, 57, 139

Tomatoes, 17, 25, 36, 49, 53, 59, 61, 100–102, 113, 126–127, 128, 129, 131; chutney, 135; under glass, 102; yields, 60

Tools, 28–29; care of, 7, 24, 29, 30

Toolshed, 24, 25, 30

Top-dressing, 16, 27, 42, 43, 140

Topsoil, 34

Trace elements, 17, 42, 43

Transplanting, 17

Transport, 14

Tree roots, 20

Trenching, 17, 34–35

Trowel, see Hand trowel

Trusses, 17, 100

Tubers, 17, 82

Turnips, 23, 39, 48–50, 60, 61, 78, 126–127, 129

V

Vegetable marrows, See Marrows

Ventilation of greenhouse, 41

W

Walnuts, pickling, 135

Water butt, 30, 43

Watering, 9, 37, 39, 45, 56, 57, 59, 110

Watering can, 28, 30

Water supply, 14, 15, 25

Weather, 7, 30, 40, 110; and harvesting, 59

Weedkiller, 23

Weeds, 12, 17, 20, 21, 22–23, 27, 28, 33, 34, 37, 39, 77

Wheelbarrow, 24, 25, 28

White currants, 120–121, 123

Wind, 38

Windbreaks, 33

Wireworms, 80, 81, 111, 113

Woodlice, 7, 111

Y

Yields, 60–61, 138–139

Youth garden programme, 13